ACCESS AWARD IN BUSINESS SKILLS

STUDY TEXT 2018

Qualifications and Credit Framework

AAT Level 1

British Library Cataloguing-in-Publication Data

A catalogue record for this book is available from the British Library.

Published by
Kaplan Publishing UK
Unit 2, The Business Centre
Molly Millars Lane
Wokingham
Berkshire
RG41 2QZ

ISBN 978 1 78740 039 9

Kaplan Publishing would like to thank Angela Renshaw and Deborah Seed for their contributions towards the production of this publication.

CONTENTS

ACCESS AWARD IN BUSINESS SKILLS STUDY TEXT

Mock Assessments

Index

INTRODUCTION

HOW TO USE THESE MATERIALS

These Kaplan Publishing learning materials have been carefully designed to make your learning experience as easy as possible and to give you the best chance of success in your AAT assessments.

They contain a number of features to help you in the study process.

The sections on the Unit Guide, the Assessment and Study Skills should be read before you commence your studies.

They are designed to familiarise you with the nature and content of the assessment and to give you tips on how best to approach your studies.

STUDY TEXT

This Study Text has been specially prepared for the revised AAT Access qualification introduced in 2018.

It is written in a practical and interactive style by expert classroom tutors.

In this Study Text:

- key terms and concepts are clearly defined

- all topics are illustrated with practical examples with clearly worked solutions based on sample tasks provided by the AAT in the new assessment style

- frequent activities throughout and at the end of the chapters ensure that what you have learnt is regularly reinforced

- 'Test your understanding' activities are included within each chapter to apply your learning and develop your understanding

- a 'Case Study' brings the subject to life and puts the content covered into a real life context

- Mock Assessments and end of chapter activities reinforce understanding to prepare you for the assessment.

ICONS

The chapters include the following icons throughout.

They are designed to assist you in your studies by identifying key definitions and the points at which you can test yourself on the knowledge gained.

 Definition

These sections explain important areas of Knowledge which must be understood and reproduced in an assessment

 Example

The illustrative examples can be used to help develop an understanding of topics before attempting the activity exercises

 Test your understanding

These are exercises which give the opportunity to assess your understanding of all the assessment areas.

 Case study

These examples put the chapter content into a real life context, using the case study of Jessica and her role at How Two Ltd.

 Case study activities

Following the chapter summary, these questions enable further practice using the real life context of the above case study.

KAPLAN PUBLISHING

UNIT GUIDE

Introduction

The AAT Access Award in Business Skills offers students at Level 1 the opportunity to develop key practical skills used in every business as a route into employment. On completion of this qualification, students will also be equipped with a strong foundation from which to progress to further study with AAT in either accountancy or bookkeeping if they would like to do so.

Students should choose to study the AAT Access Award in Business Skills to help them develop their employability skills and prepare for the workplace. Students will develop their basic numeracy skills to support everyday business activities, which will also be of use in their activities outside work. Students will also gain a practical understanding of how money moves in business and the processes and procedures that control the sales and purchases processes.

The AAT Access Award in Business Skills introduces students to the world of work and develops their employability skills. The qualification covers a range of skills and the relevant supporting knowledge in three mandatory units:

* Preparing for Work
* Using Numbers in Business
* Sales and Purchases in Business

A student completing this qualification will develop an understanding of how different organisations operate, across both the public and private sectors. They will learn how to contribute effectively in the workplace by working with others, managing their time, behaving professionally and maintaining security of data. Students will develop the skills to identify jobs that match their skills and abilities and to apply for a job using an application form or C.V.

Studying this qualification will also equip students with the basic numerical skills needed in the workplace, and in life outside work. These numerical skills range from simple calculations that are used most often in business to working with decimals, percentages and fractions, and applying proportions and ratios.

On completion of this qualification, students will also have gained an understanding of the ways in which businesses process sales and purchases and the documentation and procedures used to move goods and services between businesses.

Mandatory units – overview and learning outcomes

Preparing for work

Overview

This unit will help students to prepare to seek employment in a wide range of sectors and to develop the skills that they need to contribute effectively in the workplace. Students will explore the key features of different types of organisations and the sectors in which they operate. They will learn the purpose of different organisations and how they operate, and also how organisations are commonly structured.

On completion of this unit, students will understand the skills needed in the workplace, including the importance of team working, effective time management and the need for professional behaviour. They will explore workplace communications and the use of software for different business tasks, while understanding the need for data security and learning how to keep data secure. Finally, students will explore how to search for and identify a suitable job and then to complete a job application.

This unit will develop practical skills that students need to seek work and to be successful in the workplace once they are employed. Learning how organisations operate will help students to better understand the processes they will explore in Sales and Purchases in Business and will be of benefit in completing documents used in the sales and purchase processes.

Learning outcomes

1. Understand how organisations operate

2. Develop skills for the workplace

3. Be able to apply for a job

Using Numbers in Business

Overview

Numeracy is an essential business skill and helps an employee to operate more effectively in any workplace. However, students will also encounter many situations outside work where basic numeracy is required.

On completion of this unit, students will have the skills to practically apply a range of common numerical methods to everyday business situations, whatever their role and regardless of the type of organisation in which they might work. They will be able to record and sort numbers, to identify differences between figures and to complete simple calculations. Students will be able to work out averages, use time and currency in calculations that support everyday business activities and work with more complex calculations, including those involving common decimals, fractions, percentages and proportions.

As basic numeracy is a key skill that employers look for when recruiting, this unit supports Preparing for Work. Being able to work with numbers also supports Sales and Purchases in Business, as students will need to understand payment terms and complete documents used in the sales and purchases processes.

Learning outcomes

1. Work with numbers

2. Perform simple business calculations

3. Work with common decimals, fractions, percentages, proportions and ratios

Sales and Purchases in Business

Overview

This unit focuses on organisations that aim to make a profit rather than those operating in the not-for-profit or public sector. Studying this unit will help students to understand the importance of sales and purchases, and the procedures that support them, to the success of those businesses.

Students will discover that businesses need to make more sales (income) than purchases (expenses) to operate profitably. Students will become familiar with the relevant terminology and common documents used. They will gain the skills necessary to perform practical finance-related tasks while following business procedures.

On completion of this unit, students will understand that businesses make money by selling goods and services. Students will also understand that businesses have to use their income to pay for the costs of running the business. They will know the processes involved in making both sales and purchases and will understand how they can contribute to the success of a business by following business procedures accurately and on time.

This unit shows the movement of money across a business by drawing on the understanding of how organisations operate that students developed in Preparing for Work. In addition, the numerical skills developed in Using Numbers in Business will help students to complete documents used in the sales and purchases processes and to understand the effects of payment terms.

Learning outcomes

1. Understand how sales and purchases support business

2. Understand principles of sales and purchases

3. Apply business procedures to sales and purchases

Scope of content and assessment criteria

Preparing for work

1. **Understand how organisations operate (Chapter 1)**

1.1 Key features of different sectors

Students need to know:

- the key features of the retail sector:
- the key features of the manufacturing sector
- the key features of the service sector
- the key features of the charity sector
- the key features of the public sector.

1.2 Purpose of different types of organisations

Students need to know:

- that some organisations are run for profit:
  - sole trader
  - partnership
  - private limited company
- that some organisations are not run for profit:
  - charity
  - public sector.

1.3 Structure of an organisation

Students need to know:

- typical departments within an organisation and what they do:
  - production
  - despatch
  - finance
  - sales and marketing
  - information and communication technology (ICT)
  - human resources
- the structure of a three-level organisation chart:
  - directors
  - department managers
  - department staff
- levels of responsibility in an organisation and who each level reports to (reporting lines):
  - director
  - manager
  - staff.

2.   Develop skills for the workplace (Chapters 4 and 5)

2.1   Working with others

Students need to know:

- the characteristics of effective team working:
    - leadership
    - clear roles and responsibilities
    - respect
    - trust
    - co-operation
    - common goals
    - realistic deadlines
    - good communication
- the importance to a team of achieving goals:
    - team morale
    - success of the organisation.

2.2   Time management

Students need to know:

- how to use planning aids to manage their time:
    - calendars
    - diaries
    - work schedules
    - to-do lists
    - checklists
- the effect on others of failing to meet a deadline
- that work might be allocated based on how urgent and important it is and who has asked for it to be carried out.

2.3   Professional behaviour

Students need to know:

- that they will be required to follow policies and procedures:
    - use of social media
    - use of personal phones
    - dress codes
    - answering business phone calls
- principles of good time keeping:
    - being at work on time
    - keeping to break times
    - not leaving early
- principles of polite communication with colleagues and customers:
    - using correct names
    - listening to the other person
    - avoiding slang, swearing and offensive humour
    - using 'please' and 'thank you'.

2.4 Workplace communications

Students need to know:

- methods of workplace communications:
  - emails
  - letters
  - reports
  - spreadsheets
  - telephone calls
  - face-to-face
  - instant messaging
- software for workplace communications:
  - word processing
  - spreadsheet
  - email
  - presentation.

2.5 Understand the importance of keeping data and information secure

Students need to know:

- why it is important to make sure that data and information is secure:
  - prevents loss and unauthorised sharing of information
  - protects against computer failure or viruses
  - maintains confidentiality
  - protects customer information
  - complies with any legal requirements
- how data and information is kept secure:
  - passwords
  - backups
  - restricted access (both electronic and physical)
  - anti-virus software.

3. Be able to apply for a job (Chapter 2)

3.1 Identifying a suitable job

Students need to know:

- where to look for job vacancies:
  - newspapers
  - recruitment agencies
  - job centre
  - apprenticeship providers
  - personal contacts
  - recruitment websites
  - social media
- how to identify requirements of job vacancies:
  - skills
  - personal qualities

- knowledge
- qualifications
- experience
- interests
- how to decide suitability for a job vacancy:
    - essential requirements
    - desirable requirements
    - suitability of applicant for job vacancy based on requirements.

3.2 Applying for a job using an application form or CV (curriculum vitae)

Students need to know:

- to include accurate personal details:
    - current contact details
    - job history
    - qualifications
    - relevant interests and experience
- the importance of:
    - checking the application
    - checking spelling
    - having the application checked by someone else
    - submitting the application by the closing date.

Using Numbers in Business

1. Work with numbers (Chapter 3)

1.1 Record and sort whole numbers

Students must be able to:

- record numbers in words and figures
- arrange numbers, including positive and negative numbers, in ascending and descending order
- identify highest number
- identify lowest number
- calculate range
- identify most frequently occurring number or numbers (mode).

2. Perform simple business calculations (Chapter 3)

2.1 Check results of calculations

Students need to know:

- how to use estimation/rounding
- how to estimate highest and lowest possible results
- how to use cross-checking.

2.2 Identify differences between figures over time

Students must be able to:

- identify increases
- identify decreases.

2.3 Complete calculations

Students must be able to:

- use numerical functions:
  - addition
  - subtraction
  - multiplication
  - division
  - calculate average (mean)
- work with common units of time
- work with common units of currency.

3. Work with common decimals, fractions, percentages, proportions and ratios (Chapter 3)

3.1 Calculate decimals, fractions and percentages of numbers

Students must be able to:

- calculate decimals
- calculate simple fractions
- calculate whole percentages
- calculate figures using whole percentages
- express a number as a fraction or percentage of another.

3.2 Calculate equivalent fractions, percentages and decimals

Students must be able to:

- convert fractions into percentages and decimals
- convert percentages into fractions and decimals
- convert decimals into percentages and fractions.

3.3 Calculate and apply simple proportions and ratios

Students must be able to:

- express one number as a proportion of another
- express two numbers as a ratio
- apply a proportion or ratio to a number.

3.4 Round numbers

Students must be able to:

- round results of calculations to whole numbers
- round results of calculations to two decimal places.

Sales and Purchases in Business

1. Understand how sales and purchases support businesses (Chapter 6)

1.1 Sales and purchases in business

Students need to know:

- The importance of sales and purchases:
  - businesses need money to operate
  - selling goods and services makes money (income)
  - buying goods and services costs money (expenses)
  - businesses need more income than expenses to run profitably
  - the meaning of profit and loss: income minus expenses
- possible problems when there is more expenditure than income:
  - not enough money to pay for purchases
  - bank account may become overdrawn
  - suppliers may withdraw credit
  - business could fail
- possible opportunities when there is more income than expenditure:
  - saving opportunity
  - business growth.

2. Understand principles of sales and purchases (Chapter 6, 7)

2.1 Sales

Students need to know:

- who goods or services are sold to:
  - customers
  - clients.
- that some sales are made on a cash basis (income is received at the same time as the sale of goods or services)
- that some sales are made on a credit basis (income is received in an agreed period of time
- after the sale of goods or services).

2.2 Purchases

Students need to know:

- who goods or services are bought from: suppliers
- that some purchases are made on a cash basis (payment is made at time of receiving goods or services)
- that some purchases are made on a credit basis (payment is made in an agreed period of time after receiving goods or services)
- that businesses may have a list of approved suppliers.

2.3 Payment terms

Students need to know:

- the purpose of payment terms:
  - to ensure that customers know when to pay their invoices

- to ensure that suppliers are paid at the agreed time.
- common terminology:
    - payment in advance
    - payment on delivery
    - payment 10, 14, 30 or 60 days after invoice date
    - payment at end of the month of invoice.
- how payment terms offered to customers/clients and received from suppliers affect the bank balance.

3. Apply business procedures to sales and purchases (Chapter 7-9)

3.1 Business procedures for sales and purchases

Students need to know:

- why it is important to follow business procedures
- how to follow procedures
- documents used in the sales process:
    - customer order
    - delivery note
    - sales invoice
- documents used in the purchase process:
    - approved supplier list
    - purchase order
    - delivery note
    - goods received note (GRN)
    - purchase invoice
- the process of making sales
- the process of purchasing goods or services

Students must be able to:

- complete documents used in the sales process (delivery note, sales invoice) with:
    - date
    - purchase order number
    - delivery note number
    - customer name and address
    - description and quantity of goods or services
    - value of goods or services including item price
    - amounts (net, VAT and total)
- select an approved supplier for specified goods or services
- complete documents used in the purchase process (purchase order, goods received note (GRN)) with:
    - date
    - purchase order number
    - supplier name and address
    - description and quantity of goods or services

- value of goods or services including item price
- amounts (net, VAT and total)
- check for differences between documents in the purchase process (purchase order, goods
  - received note (GRN), delivery note):
  - incorrect items or quantity of goods
  - items missing from delivery
  - incorrect item price
  - incorrect calculations.

The assessment

Assessment for this award will be by Computer based assessment (CBA), with a mixture of computer-marked tasks, including multiple choice, true/false, drag and drop, drop-down lists, calculation and completion of relevant forms.

The assessment will be under timed conditions. The timed allowed for the assessment is 90 minutes.

The assessment is wholly computer-marked.

The weighting of the learning outcomes is as follows:

Preparing for Work
1. Understand how organisations operate	10%
2. Develop skills for the workplace	10%
3. Be able to apply for a job	10%

Using Numbers in Business
1. Work with numbers	5%
2. Perform simple business calculations	10%
3. Work with common decimals, fractions, percentages, proportions & ratios	15%

Sales and Purchases in Business
1. Understand how sales and purchases support businesses	5%
2. Understand principles of sales and purchases	10%
3. Apply business procedures to sales and purchases	15%

Integration	10%
Total	100%

STUDY SKILLS

Preparing to study

Devise a study plan

Determine which times of the week you will study.

Split these times into sessions of at least one hour for study of new material. Any shorter periods could be used for revision or practice.

Put the times you plan to study onto a study plan for the weeks from now until the assessment and set yourself targets for each period of study – in your sessions make sure you cover the whole course, activities and the associated questions with answers at the back of the Study Text.

When working through your course, compare your progress with your plan and, if necessary, re-plan your work (perhaps including extra sessions) or, if you are ahead, do some extra revision/practice questions.

Effective studying

Active reading

You are not expected to learn the text by rote, rather, you must understand what you are reading and be able to use it to pass the assessment and develop good practice.

A good technique is to use SQ3Rs – Survey, Question, Read, Recall, Review:

1 **Survey the chapter**

   Look at the headings and read the introduction, knowledge, skills and content, so as to get an overview of what the chapter deals with.

2 **Question**

   Whilst undertaking the survey ask yourself the questions you hope the chapter will answer for you.

3 **Read**

   Read through the chapter thoroughly working through the activities and, at the end, making sure that you can meet the learning objectives shown within the summary.

4 **Recall**

   At the end of each chapter, try to recall the main ideas of the section/chapter without referring to the text. This is best done after short break of a couple of minutes after the reading stage.

5 **Review**

   Check that your recall notes are correct.

You may also find it helpful to re-read the chapter to try and see the topic(s) it deals with as a whole.

Note taking

Taking notes is a useful way of learning, but do not simply copy out the text. The notes must:

- be in your own words
- be concise
- cover the key points
- be well organised
- be modified as you study further chapters in this text or in related ones.

Trying to summarise a chapter without referring to the text can be a useful way of determining which areas you know and which you don't.

Three ways of taking notes

1   **Summarise the key points of a chapter**

2   **Make linear notes**

A list of headings, subdivided with sub-headings listing the key points.

If you use linear notes, you can use different colours to highlight key points and keep topic areas together.

Use plenty of space to make your notes easy to use.

3   **Try a diagrammatic form**

The most common of which is a mind map.

To make a mind map, put the main heading in the centre of the paper and put a circle around it.

Draw lines radiating from this to the main sub-headings which again have circles around them.

Continue the process from the sub-headings to sub-sub-headings.

Highlighting and underlining

You may find it useful to underline or highlight key points in your study text – but do be selective.

You may also wish to make notes in the margins.

Further reading

In addition to this text, you should also read the 'Student section' of the 'Accounting Technician' magazine every month to keep abreast of any guidance from the examiners.

KAPLAN PUBLISHING

How organisations operate

1

Introduction

There are different types of business organisations, each having their own agenda and objectives.

In this chapter you will learn about the various types of business organisations and how they operate.

KNOWLEDGE	CONTENTS
Prepare for work	1 The key features of an organisation
1.1 Key features of different sectors	2 The structure of an organisation
1.2 Purpose of different types of organisations	3 Summary and further questions
1.3 Structure of an organisation	4 Answers to chapter questions

1 The key features of an organisation

1.1 Case study: an introduction

 Case study

Jessica has decided that she has had enough of full time education.

She wants a career and at the same time she needs to earn some money. After careful consideration and following discussions with a careers advisor, Jessica thinks that an apprenticeship would be the best way forward for her.

As Jessica is unsure of the type of career that she would like train for, she has decided to investigate different kinds of organisations to gain an insight into how they worked and possibly identify something that she would enjoy.

Jessica is aware that there are many different business sectors and starts by looking at each in turn.

1.2 The different sectors within business

There are many different sectors in the world of business. You need to know what these are and how to differentiate between them.

 Definitions

The retail sector sells goods to the public.

The manufacturing sector makes products to sell to the public or as components for further manufacturing.

The service sector provides services rather than manufacturing or selling goods.

The charity sector generates income to support its purpose.

The public sector provides services to the public. These services are funded by the Government with money generated through taxes.

The private sector includes profit making organisations. This can be a sole trader working alone or they may have employees. There are also partnerships and limited companies in the private sector.

KAPLAN PUBLISHING

1.3   The retail sector

The retail sector includes any organisation (typically shops) selling goods to the general public.

On a local level, this includes any small shop (for example, a grocer or a newsagent).

Other retailers, such as some large supermarkets and retail outlets, have several branches throughout the country and many even have stores worldwide (for example, Tesco and Marks and Spencer).

There is an increasing trend towards buying goods online, including groceries and household essentials. The majority of large stores and supermarkets have an online shopping facility, including 'Click and Collect' services where a customer can order their products on a website and then go to a shop or collection point to obtain their purchases. Other companies specialise in online sales and have a minimal high street or physical presence (for example, Amazon and clothes retailers such as ASOS).

The retail sector also includes franchises. A franchise is where the owner of the business (franchisor) sells rights to a third party (franchisee). These rights include the ability to use their logo, sell their products or services and use their system of doing business. The franchisor receives ongoing royalties from the franchisee. Lots of well-known fast food companies are franchises (for example, Subway and McDonald's).

1.4   The manufacturing sector

The manufacturing sector includes businesses ranging from a small company with a few employees on the production line to large factories with hundreds of employees.

Their primary concern is manufacturing and they can produce anything, whether that is goods to go on sale to the public or components for further manufacture.

 Examples

For example, a clothing factory will produce completed garments to supply to retail outlets for direct sale to the general public.

Whereas, a car manufacturing company only actually has an assembly line. The components that go in to assembling a car will have been produced in different factories, therefore these would be classed as components for further manufacture.

1.5   The service sector

The service sector provides services that do not involve the manufacture or selling of goods.

These businesses do not focus on the supply of physical products and instead seek to provide advice or a service to the customer or user.

 Examples

Buses, trains and trams all provide the public with a transport service. Road haulage is another service, trucks transport goods around the country, some even travel abroad to export goods to retailers.

Banks provide a financial service.

Solicitors provide a legal service.

1.6   The charity sector

The charity sector raises money for causes in various ways. Charities are not-for-profit organisations meaning that they do not make a profit, instead using any money made to achieve the organisation's objectives.

Charities are governed by specific legislation such as the Charities Act 2011 and Charities (Social and protection) Act 2016.

Some charities have high street shops selling goods donated by the public. Donations are all voluntary, as is the time given by most staff working in the charity shops. However, most charity shop managers are paid a wage.

Money is raised through a variety of methods in the charity sector: donations in envelopes from the public, television campaigns and collection boxes in stores are just some of the other ways this is achieved.

 Examples

There are many charities helping various causes such as:

Animal welfare (RSCPA, Blue Cross)

Disaster relief and humanitarian causes (British Red Cross, UNICEF)

Health and age-related issues (Age UK, Cancer Research, Guide Dogs for the Blind)

Young people at home and abroad (Barnardo's, Save the Children)

Activity

Write down the names of as many charities you can think of.

Then, write down what you think each charity does for the public or for the 'common good' of society.

Then check their websites to see if what they do is what you think they do.

1.7   The public sector

The public sector provides services that are essential to the population, such as education and health care.

They are funded by the Government using monies raised through taxation and are not-for-profit organisations.

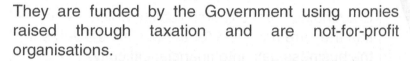 **Examples**

Public sector organisations include the NHS (National Health Service), Police, Ambulance and Fire Brigade.

1.8   The private sector

The private sector is made up of organisations aiming to make profit for the owner/owners.

These may be sole traders, partnerships or private limited companies, all of which are described in the chart below.

Type of Business	Ownership
Sole Trader	A sole trader business is owned by one person. If the business makes a profit the owner will keep all the profits. However, if the business gets into financial difficulty, the sole trader is responsible for all the debts. A sole trader may work on their own or have several employees. The owner is in direct control of all elements and is legally accountable for the finances of the business. Sole traders may use a trade name or business name other than their own legal name.

Partnership	A partnership is similar to a sole trader business but is owned by between two and twenty people.
	Each partner will take a share of the profits of the business or be liable for the losses of the business.
Limited companies	When a limited company is set up it is given its own legal identity. The ownership of these companies is divided into shares of the business. Any profit made by the business is allocated to shareholders in the form of dividends, based on how many shares they hold.
	Shareholders have limited liability which means that they are not liable for the business's debts. If the business gets into financial difficulty, shareholders only lose the money they invested.
	The shares of private limited companies (Ltd) are usually given to the directors of the organisation or other private individuals.
	The shares of public limited companies (plc) are sold on the stock exchange which means that anyone from the general public can buy them.

📝 Test your understanding 1

Match the different sectors to the key features of organisations within each. Put a tick in the correct box.

	Transports people	Makes products	Upholds the law	Provides aid	Sells goods	Makes profit
Retail						
Manufacturing						
Service						
Charity						
Public						
Private						

Test your understanding 2

Are the following types of organisations profit or not-for-profit organisations? Tick the correct box for each.

	Profit	Not-for-profit
Retail		
Manufacturing		
Service		
Charity		
Public		
Private		

Test your understanding 3

Complete the sentences below using the pick list provided.

_____ sector organisations are normally concerned with the provision of basic government services.

_____ are private businesses owned by one person.

_____ sector organisations are primarily concerned with making profit from the sale of goods or services. Where these businesses have shareholders they are known as _____.

Pick list

Private	Public	Charity
Sole traders	Partnerships	Limited companies

Test your understanding 4

Identify the purpose of each sector by matching the sector in the first column with the purpose in the second column.

Sector	Purpose
Manufacturing Sector	To provide essential services
Private Sector	To promote a cause
Public Sector	To produce goods and components
Charity Sector	To make a profit

 Test your understanding 5

Below are six descriptions of what different organisations do. Match the description to the relevant sector from those provided by placing a tick in the relevant box.

	Sells furniture	Is a sole trader	Animal welfare	Offers financial advice	Provides education	Makes zips for clothes
Retail						
Manufacturing						
Service						
Charity						
Private						
Public						

2 The structure of an organisation

2.1 The structure of an organisation

 Definition

Organisational structure is concerned with the way in which work is divided up and allocated. It outlines the roles and responsibilities of individuals and groups within an organisation. As such, each organisation's structure will be slightly different to another's.

Within each organisation, there will be several different departments, all performing various functions and with separate areas of expertise and unique responsibilities.

The exact nature of these departments and the way they relate to each other and contribute to the organisation will vary for each sector, so we will consider each in turn before identifying common features for all sectors.

 Definition

Function – an activity carried out in an organisation. For example, the accounting function is carried out by the staff in the accounts department.

2.2 Typical departments in retail

In retail, the size of the store determines how many departments it has. A small store such as a speciality shop or newsagents does not have various departments (this will be explored later in the chapter).

Therefore, we are going to concentrate on the larger retail outlets. This would include any high street clothing or homeware shop with multiple sites, as well as supermarkets and department stores.

Key departments for these organisations typically include:

- Item-specific product areas – different sections relating to the type of goods on sale for example food, clothing, alcohol, tools etc.

- Cashiers – to collect money from the customer

- Shelf-stackers and stock controllers – to monitor and replenish stock sold

- Finance – to handle all accountancy services including the handling of all bookkeeping transactions and payables and receivables. Also usually responsible for payroll and the use of accounting software for the management of financial data and costing using spreadsheets.

  However, the cash flow of a large store is usually also monitored throughout the day. Cashiers have to sign into a cash register, making them responsible for any shortfall in takings while they are using that till. Any refunds or voiding of a transaction has to be authorised by a store supervisor. When there is a change in cashier the cash register can be emptied and the takings counted. Collectively at the end of the working day all cash register takings are added together giving the total sales figure for the day.

- Sales and marketing – to ensure retail sales through methods such as advertising and promotions including discounts on goods. Some product ranges (e.g. food and cosmetics) can be promoted in store where customers are invited to try small samples in an attempt to entice them to buy the product. Catalogues or leaflets are often used to promote sales. This department usually monitors consumer trends and aims to meet supply and demand.

- Despatch and receipt of goods – to arrange the delivery and storage of stock. Large stores have storage facilities that not only receive goods for sale but also have to despatch goods to customers buying from the internet or mail order.

- Administration – to sort documentation and maintain records, including filing to assist other departments such as finance and despatch. This department is also typically responsible for the ordering and allocation of supplies such as stationery and all tasks relating to the organisation of meetings within the business.

- I.T. – to monitor all daily operations in store, including stock, ordering and purchasing, wages, cash registers, supply chains, cross-company stock inventory, training needs of personnel and communication between departments. This department is of vital importance in the retail sector.

- Human Resources (H.R.) – responsible for recruitment, traditionally they screen, interview and place workers into suitable roles. However, in recent times the staff in this department are part of an interview panel whereby the manager/supervisor of a department may be involved with the interview. H.R may also be responsible for training, compensation, safety, benefits and payroll.

Note: While small retailers do not have different departments, and tend to self - manage the day to day running of the business, they usually employ an accountant to do their bookkeeping and ensure that all their finances are accurate and up to date.

2.3   Typical departments in manufacturing

Unlike the retail sector, the manufacturing sector relies heavily on the operating of equipment and therefore many of the departments relate to the production process.

- Production – where employees make the goods or components. This usually relies on the use of machinery.

- Maintenance – machines can develop faults. The maintenance department will have personnel such as engineers, fitters and electricians. Some machines are operated by computer systems rather than people and if these develop a fault an I.T. technician needs to diagnose and rectify the problem.

- Packaging – once the goods have been made they are packaged and stored ready to be delivered to the customer.

- Despatch – responsible for the timely distribution of goods. This is usually by road transport but can also be by rail (e.g. in quarries where products such as lime and aggregates are loaded into goods trains).

- Finance – as in the retail sector, this comprises of accountancy staff responsible for all bookkeeping, payroll, costing and the use of accounting software for the management of financial data.

- Sales and Marketing – promotes the sales of goods by advertising, telephone, the internet and visiting potential customers to show their product. Many manufacturers also use third party sales agencies or wholesalers/resellers to generate sales.

- I.T. – most companies in this sector have an internal computer program application, accessible to authorised personnel. All departments listed will have an authorised user. Computer systems can track productivity at every level and are a useful tool in communication between departments.

- Administration – as in the retail sector, this department is responsible for maintaining records, organising office supplies and other clerical support for other departments and senior management.

- Human Resources (H.R.) – as in the retail sector, this department is responsible for recruitment and staff training and welfare.

2.4 Typical departments in the service sector

The service sector by definition is a very broad spectrum term, many organisations fall into this category. It is therefore impractical to list them all and their departments.

The following overview of some organisations should assist in identifying the structure of most service sectors.

Transport services

This includes buses, trains, trams and aeroplanes, all of which provide the transportation of passengers to a destination of their choice. The key departments include:

- Transport – not only to enable the customer to complete their journey, but also trucks, vans and planes to transport other goods

- Planning – the creation and monitoring of routes and timetables

- Maintenance – all transport needs to be maintained and repaired where necessary. Each area of transport has workshops where the maintenance/repairs can be carried out by personnel with the necessary skills to complete the work needed.

- Drivers/Pilots – to fulfil the requirements necessary of their chosen career in order to be able to transport passengers. Similarly, a special licence has to be obtained to transport goods or passengers.

- Ticket sales – Passengers can purchase tickets in various ways such as online, a ticket office, aboard the transport, or a seasonal pass.

- Transport office – to take orders for deliveries, plan drivers' work and allocate routes appropriately.

- I.T. – as in the other sectors above, but also to provide information to customers and drivers, including vehicle tracking and electronic timetables.

- Administration – as in the other sectors above.

- Human Resources – as in the other sectors above.

- Finance – as in the other sectors above.

KAPLAN PUBLISHING

Banks and financial services

Conversely, banks are part of the service sector, departments within a bank include:

- Lending

- Saving

- Investment

- Credit Cards

- Customer Service

- I.T – as in the other sectors above, but including online banking services.

- Administration – as in the other sectors above.

- Human Resources – as in the other sectors above.

2.5 Typical departments in the charity sector

Although the nature of the charity's primary fundraising activities will to some extent determine the staff and departments it will have, the following functions would be common to most charities:

- Head Office – co-ordinates and allocates income generated

- Fund-raising – devise ways of generating income, often including telephone and e-mail campaigns, as well as shops, collection boxes and other specialist functions below.

- Shops – take in goods donated by the public and sell them back to the public to generate funds

- Collection boxes – are distributed throughout the country usually in large stores for the public to donate cash. Their periodic collection and processing require co-ordination.

- Online – various ways of donating online, some people complete tasks such as long walks, long distance swimming etc. and ask people to sponsor them with the proceeds going to a pre-chosen charity.

- Human Resources - as in the other sectors above.

- Finance – as in the other sectors above, including payroll for those who do receive a wage.

2.6 Typical departments in the public sector

There are many public services, all of which have one thing in common. They are controlled by the government.

They are given a specific budget and are expected to adhere to it. The government can impose penalties for overspending or contravening rules.

If we consider some of the main public sector organisations, each will have their own specialist departments, as follows:

- The N.H.S. – Providing healthcare

- Police – Upholding the law and protecting the public

- Fire Service – Extinguishing fires and rescuing people in various situations such as accidents

- Ambulance Service – Treating the sick and injured on scene and transporting them to hospital

Each of the public sector services mentioned above will have the following departments in addition to their main services:

- Finance – accountants responsible for bookkeeping, costing, payroll, etc.

- I.T. – each government department has internal I.T systems that can be accessed by staff. Most staff have access to specific areas of the system and have passwords that will allow them to access the area that they are authorised to use. The I.T department is usually large and employs many technicians to keep the system updated and running smoothly.

- Complaints - all government services have a complaints department.

2.7 Typical departments in the private sector

The departments present in private sector organisations will largely overlap with those in the retail, manufacturing or service sectors dependent on what the business does to make profit.

A large online retailer, a manufacturer of electrical components and an insurance company would all be considered to be in the private sector and although each would have specialist departments, most would share common departments such as administration, sales and marketing, product-specific groups, despatch/transportation, research/development, I.T., finance and human resources (H.R.).

Let us consider one type of business in the private sector which would not necessarily have as many specialist departments, sole traders. Returning to the overlap with the retail sector, most small shops are usually sole traders in business. Their primary aim, as with any organisation in the private sector, is to make a profit. However, unlike some of the earlier examples of private sector businesses and the previous illustration of a larger retail company, they do not have separate in-store departments.

 Example

A small shop selling a mixture of goods:

- Owner – works in the shop and is responsible for day-to-day operations, including acting as the principal cashier.

- Shop assistant(s) – also serve customers and act as cashier(s).

- Owner acquires own goods – goes to the cash and carry to collect goods to sell on to customers.

- Owner sells and promotes own goods.

- Owner performs most Human Resources tasks including conducting own interviews, recruitment and training.

- Finance – owner employs an accountant to ensure finances are up to date and accurate; the accountant also works out the employee's wages.

2.8 A common factor for all organisations

Accountancy is a service provided to anyone who requires expert financial assistance. It is apparent that all organisations in any sector need this service to ensure that their finances are in order and that they are complying with the necessary finance legislation.

Test your understanding 6

Show the purpose of each department by placing a tick in the relevant box.

	Sells to the consumer and advertises promotions	Responsible for the computer hardware and software in a business	Deals with the recording and processing of financial transactions	Packages and stores the goods before despatch	Makes components for further assembly
IT					
Production					
Sales and marketing					
Packaging					
Finance					

2.9 The hierarchy of an organisation

 Definition

The hierarchy of an organisation describes the way that responsibility is distributed between different levels of an organisation, in terms of the status of the employee rather than their department or function.

The internal structure of an organisation, and the number of levels of responsibility, can therefore vary dependent on its size.

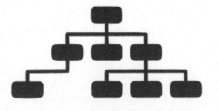

For example, every large organisation has a Chief Executive Officer (CEO) who has the responsibility for the overall success of an entire organisation. Their role within companies and public or private-sector organisations includes planning, directing and coordinating operational activities. They also devise policies and strategies to ensure that organisations meet their goals. For the purpose of this chapter we will look at the structure of an organisation below this level.

Smaller organisations have directors and managers who perform similar roles to a CEO. Let us then consider a three-level organisation, with directors, managers and employees.

Example

A three-level organisation:

Director(s)

Overall responsibility for the day to day running of an organisation, strategies, finances, decision making, planning, delegation, leadership, problem solving, overseeing other departments

Department Manager(s)

Delegation of duties, oversees staff, ensuring that employees are performing their duties correctly and in a timely manner, promotes productivity, problem solving, ensures that staff have all the tools/equipment necessary to fulfil their role, time management.

Reports any problems/issues that they are unable to solve to the Director unless it is a specific problem with a member of staff, in which circumstances, Human Resources may be asked to be involved.

Department Staff

Carry out all duties expected of them in a timely and efficient manner.

Pay attention to detail and deadlines.

Report any problems to their line manager.

Test your understanding 7

Place these job titles in the correct order, with the most senior person at the top and the least senior person at the bottom.

Person	Hierarchy
Department staff	
Department manager	
Director	

Test your understanding 8

Place these job titles in the correct order, with the most senior person at the top and the least senior person at the bottom.

Person	Description
Department staff	Carry out all duties expected of them
Department manager	Overall responsibility for the day to day running of an organisation
Director	Oversees staff, ensuring that employees are performing their duties correctly

3 Summary and further questions

You should now be able to identify different types of organisation, the sector in which they operate and the departments necessary to allow them to function effectively. You should also have an understanding of how these organisations may be organised internally and how responsibility is distributed between different types of employee.

You should also be able to identify which organisations are run to make a profit or those which are not-for-profit organisations.

Let us return to the case study for further questions relating to the topics covered.

Case study activity 1

To help with her research, Jessica thinks about the local companies her friends and family work for.

- Her father is a financial advisor for the Owlsmoor Building Society
- Her mother is a fundraiser for the Cheshire Dogs Trust
- Her best friend is a sales assistant at TZMinz, a clothes shop
- Her sister has an admin role at Rainson & Sons, a producer of plumbing parts

For each organisation, select the correct sector from the options provided. Tick the box to show the correct answer.

	Retail	Manufacturing	Service	Charity
Owlsmoor Building Society				
Cheshire Dogs Trust				
TZMinz				
Rainson & Sons				

Could any of these be considered to be public sector organisations? Tick the relevant box(es).

Owlsmoor Building Society	
Cheshire Dogs Trust	
TZMinz	
Rainson & Sons	

Case study activity 2

Jessica starts to look for jobs online.

To limit her search, she considers which department she would like to work in. Match the following definitions with the correct department to assist Jessica in her search.

Department	Definition
PRODUCTION	This department sells the company's goods and services to customers.
SALES	This department is responsible for typing, collecting and distributing mail, keeping & filing records, organising meetings and maintaining resources.
ADMINISTRATION	This department deals with the recruitment of new staff, the training of new and existing staff, pay negotiations and regular staff appraisals.
ACCOUNTING	This department is responsible for producing the goods or services that a business provides by making best use of the various inputs.
HUMAN RESOURCES	This department is responsible for keeping records and accounts, for giving advice on budgets to other departments, and for paying wages and salaries.

KAPLAN PUBLISHING

Answers to chapter activities

Test your understanding 1

	Transports people	Makes products	Upholds the law	Animal welfare	Sells goods	Makes profit
Retail					✓	
Manufacturing		✓				
Service	✓					
Charity				✓		
Public			✓			
Private						✓

Test your understanding 2

	Profit	Not-for-profit
Retail	✓	
Manufacturing	✓	
Service	✓	
Charity		✓
Public		✓
Private	✓	

Test your understanding 3

Public sector organisations are normally concerned with the provision of basic government services.

Sole traders are private businesses owned by one person.

Private sector organisations are primarily concerned with making profit from the sale of goods or services. Where these businesses have shareholders they are known as **Limited companies.**

Test your understanding 4

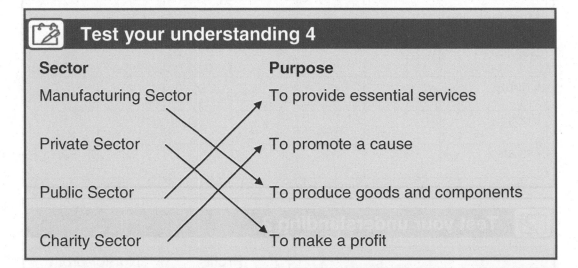

Sector	Purpose
Manufacturing Sector	To provide essential services
Private Sector	To promote a cause
Public Sector	To produce goods and components
Charity Sector	To make a profit

Test your understanding 5

	Sells furniture	Is a sole trader	Animal welfare	Offers financial advice	Provides education	Makes zips for clothes
Retail	✓					
Manufacturing						✓
Service				✓		
Charity			✓			
Private		✓				
Public					✓	

KAPLAN PUBLISHING

Test your understanding 6

	Sells to the consumer and advertises promotions	Responsible for the computer hardware and software in a business	Deals with the recording and processing of financial transactions	Packages and stores the goods before despatch	Makes components for further assembly
IT		✓			
Production					✓
Sales and marketing	✓				
Packaging				✓	
Finance			✓		

Test your understanding 7

Hierarchy

Director
Department manager
Department staff

Test your understanding 8

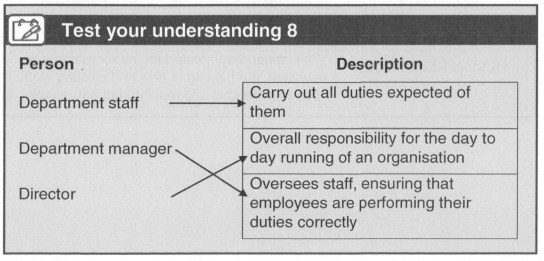

Person	Description
Department staff	Carry out all duties expected of them
Department manager	Overall responsibility for the day to day running of an organisation
Director	Oversees staff, ensuring that employees are performing their duties correctly

Case study activity 1

	Retail	Manufacturing	Service	Charity
Owlsmoor Building Society			✓	
Cheshire Dogs Trust				✓
TZMinz	✓			
Rainson & Sons		✓		

None of the organisations could be considered to be public sector.

Case study activity 2

Department	Definition
PRODUCTION	This department is responsible for producing the goods or services that a business provides by making best use of the various inputs.
SALES	This department sells the company's goods and services to customers.
ADMINISTRATION	This department is responsible for typing, collecting and distributing mail, keeping & filing records, organising meetings and maintaining resources.
ACCOUNTING	This department is responsible for keeping records and accounts, for giving advice on budgets to other departments, and for paying wages and salaries.
HUMAN RESOURCES	This department deals with the recruitment of new staff, the training of new and existing staff, pay negotiations and regular staff appraisals.

Applying for a job

2

Introduction

In this chapter you will learn where to look for a job vacancy. It is advantageous to search as many of the places suggested as possible. Restricting your search to one area such as, for example, the job centre will limit your chances of successfully identifying the right job for you. You will also learn how to apply for a job and how to prepare for a successful interview.

KNOWLEDGE	CONTENTS
Prepare for work	1 Identifying a suitable job
3.1 Identifying a suitable job	2 Applying for a job
3.2 Applying for a job using an application form or CV (Curriculum Vitae)	3 Preparing for an interview
	4 Summary and further questions

1 Identifying a suitable job

1.1 Case study: identifying a job

 Case study

Having thoroughly investigated the different organisations and looked in the local newspaper, Jessica next needed to identify which area she would like to work in.

She decided to make a list of her skills in an attempt to match herself with a suitable employment.

1.2 Where to look for job vacancies

There are many different places where job vacancies are advertised.

These include:

- **Newspapers** – both local and national newspapers have employment sections with listings of vacancies. These range from brief text listings with little information about the role to more colourful and detailed advertisements designed to make the vacancy or organisation look more appealing. Vacancies published often list the criteria expected of applicants, as well as details of location and, in some cases, the salary.

- **Recruitment agencies** – working on behalf of a number of clients, recruitment agencies match available candidates to the roles their customers need to fill. They typically charge a commission payment for this service. Recruitment agencies often have permanent positions available, although some focus on filling temporary roles or specialist areas of work (e.g. office, warehouse, accounting staff).

  For candidates seeking employment, a recruitment consultant offers a direct route to the employer and as such can adapt their application to meet the needs of each particular role.

- **Jobcentre Plus** – funded by the government, Jobcentre Plus offices are found in most cities and aim to help people of working age to find employment.

It serves as both an employment agency and a source of advice and training for job-seekers who are struggling to find a suitable role or having problems with applications and interviews. As such, it is important to not just look on the vacancy boards (now often also on touch-screen computer terminals), but also to speak to the staff working there. Having identified what a candidate is looking for, they can be very helpful.

- **Recruitment websites** – according to a report conducted by Social Talent in 2016, 26% of recruiters claim that online 'job boards' (where vacancies are listed) is their primary means of recruiting staff and it has been consistently shown that 85% of recruiters use paid online advertising to list their jobs online via one of the established sites. As well as advertising vacancies, many sites allow you to upload your C.V. and contact you if you match one of their vacancies. You may have to sign up to their website but it is free to do this.

 Examples

There are thousands of online recruitment sites and job boards operating in the UK today.

Based on site traffic, CareerExperts.co.uk suggested that the most popular in 2017 are as follows:

Indeed.co.uk – this site has over 200 million unique visitors every month from over 60 different countries.

Totaljobs.com – one of the UK's leading boards, with around 6 million job-seekers active on the site each month and 110,000 live job adverts.

Reed.co.uk – the site features open positions from over 25,000 recruiters every year and receives over 160,000 applications per day.

Monster.co.uk – one of the most established job boards, it offers a variety of services other than job searches,

CV-library.co.uk – designed to allow candidates to upload their C.V.s for employers to search, this site has over 158,000 active positions.

Jobsite.co.uk – launched 18 years ago, this site works with some of the UK's leading employers and has over 150,000 new roles each month.

- **Social media** – due to changes in technology and communication, it is now equally common for recruiters and job-seekers to connect directly online.

This can be done through a variety of social media channels, allowing employers to detail available positions on Facebook or LinkedIn, asking their contacts to share their posts. Likewise, individuals can explain the sort of roles they are looking for and ask others to share it on their personal page in case anyone with whom they are connected is recruiting.

- **Apprenticeship providers** – if you choose to undertake an apprenticeship qualification with them, most apprenticeship specialists will be able to find you employment, subject to a successful interview.

- **Personal contacts** – peak to people, tell them what you are looking for, you will be surprised what and who people know.

1.3 Identifying the requirements of job vacancies

Having explored the above sources of job vacancies, it is then necessary to break down the advertisement to see what exactly is required to be successful and, as a result, whether the role would be suitable.

Most job advertisements, whether published in a newspaper, located on a board at an employment centre or listed online, will include two key elements: a job description and a person specification.

 Definition

A job description is a broad statement of the purpose, scope, duties and responsibilities of a job.

The job description therefore outlines the tasks, daily responsibilities and overall purpose of the job. It is likely to specify where the role is located, its position within the company (including whether staff report to this person and who the person reports to) and opportunities for training and progression. Progression means the opportunity to be promoted into roles higher in the organisation or seeking new skills and responsibility for personal development elsewhere.

Employers cannot recruit effectively unless they are aware of the sort of person who would best be able to fill the role based on the job description and their understanding of the organisation. Therefore, a person specification is created.

 Definition

The person specification is a detailed illustration of the kind of person most suitable for the job. It contains a list of the attributes that the ideal candidate would possess and by which candidates for the job can be measured.

The person specification will often be the part of the job advertisement which will enable you to work out if the job is suitable.

It typically will include a list of requirements, as follows:

- **Skills** – which skills are required to be able to undertake the role that is advertised? Some of these are likely to be fairly generic and applicable to many roles (e.g. organisational skills), whereas others will be fairly unique to the role being applied for (e.g. accounting skills).

🔆 Examples

Some of the following skills are often included in job specifications:

- Organisational skills
- Written communication skills
- Verbal communication skills
- Listening skills
- Time management skills
- Problem-solving skills
- Leadership/management skills (for higher level positions)
- Mathematical skills
- IT skills
- Role-specific and technical skills (e.g. accounting, marketing)

- **Personal qualities** – different to skills, these qualities are more about how you act as a person. Ask yourself whether you feel that you have the personal qualities that are required as per the advertised role.

🔆 Examples

Some of the following personal qualities could be listed as desirable:

- Commitment and dedication – devoting your time and effort to something you believe in.
- Flexibility – adapting to situations and being able to work in different ways at different times.
- Courtesy – showing respect and being polite to others, whether they be colleagues or customers.
- Perseverance – never giving up despite difficulties and hurdles presenting themselves.
- Using initiative – taking responsibility for situations and delivering solutions.
- Being open to change and new ideas.

- **Knowledge** – do you have the relevant knowledge to be able to take on the role? Although many positions will offer adequate training, usually a level of prior knowledge will be required.

- **Qualifications** – does the role require any specific qualifications? For example, many positions will specify a certain number of GCSEs or A-Levels.

- **Experience** – do you need any previous experience to be able to apply for the role? If so, do you have this? If working in some of the departments described in Chapter 1, such as Marketing or H.R., it is often stated in the advertisement that previous experience (e.g. 'a minimum of two years') is needed.

 Case study

Although Jessica wanted to be a vet when she was younger, she would not have the knowledge, qualifications or experience to enter into this sort of role. A significant period of study at university and previous experience of working with animals would be necessary in order to perform this or similar roles.

- **Interests** – The employer will want to know a little bit about the candidates, in order to help them to assess whether they feel they will fit into their organisation.

1.4 Deciding the suitability of a job

Having examined the advertisement in depth, to establish whether or not it is suitable, it is important to establish which of the requirements are **essential** and which are **desirable**.

Essential requirements – these are skills, knowledge and attributes that are always necessary to being able to perform the advertised job vacancy.

 Example

A Senior Sales Ledger role might state that you 'must have at least 3 years' experience of working in Sales Ledger'. Other Senior Roles within accountancy might state that you must be AAT qualified meaning that you must have completed the AAT qualification up to Professional Diploma level to be able to apply for the position.

Desirable requirements – these are skills, knowledge or attributes that are relevant to the role but are not necessarily 'a must'. In other words, the successful applicant may not have these skills or experience.

Example

If applying for a position in an accountancy practice, the vacancy might state, 'desirable, knowledge of Sage One, Xero and Quickbooks'. This doesn't necessarily mean that you have to be able to use all of these packages, as training will probably be provided. However, if you do know how to use these packages it would be an advantage.

By looking at the role requirements and assessing your current level of working, you should be able to identify whether or not the role is **suitable** for you. Consider whether you have enough experience and skills to perform the duties in the job advertisement and whether or not you meet all of the essential requirements.

 Examples

If you are 16 years old and looking for an accountancy apprenticeship, you would not be applying for Management Accounts or Financial Controller positions.

If you are an experienced Assistant Store Manager for a clothing brand, you could consider applying for Store Manager jobs for other retailers. However, equally, you would not be applying for Financial Controller positions as you experience would not be relevant.

 Case study

In order for find the most suitable role for her, Jessica lists her top skills:

Enjoy mathematics, one of the best examination results - A*

Really good I.T. skills, another good examination result – A

Familiar with all MS Office programs

Can devise presentations with PowerPoint

Used Excel to make spreadsheets

Regularly use Word

Good communication skills

Confident dealing with the public, having had retail experience

Gained basic knowledge of the financial side of a business

Enjoy working with other people

Confident when working alone

Enjoy learning new skills

📝 Activity 1

Look at Jessica's list of skills and come up with your own list of your top ten skills:

1	
2	
3	
4	
5	
6	
7	
8	
9	
10	

📝 Test your understanding 1

Tick the boxes to show which skills are being shown in each example.

Example	Organisational	Written communication	Verbal communication	IT
Weekly e-mail bulletins to key clients				
Booking an off-site meeting for managers				
Creating a spreadsheet of all suppliers used by the company				
Doing a presentation on charity ideas to your department				

Test your understanding 2

The following job advertisement is showing on an online job site:

Office Manager

Tenderstem Technologies Ltd is looking to recruit a new Office Manager to co-ordinate the daily administrative operations of our food technology business.

Key responsibilities of this role include:

- the line management of three members of office staff
- co-ordination of the purchasing of office supplies
- management of the provision of administrative support to other departments
- liaison with suppliers and contractors, including maintenance and IT
- responsibility for the Health & Safety and Staff Wellbeing policies.

The following skills are essential to this position:

- superior organisation skills
- excellent verbal and written communication skills
- the ability to manage and motivate staff
- past experience of office management.

The following qualifications would be desirable, but not essential:

- A minimum of 8 GCSE's including Grade A-C English and Mathematics
- Formal Health and Safety certification.

The successful candidate need not have any experience of the food industry but should be able to show commitment, flexibility, attention to detail and a desire to improve systems. In a leadership position, this role is best suited to individuals able to make decisions alone, using their own initiative.

Salary and further details on request.

(a) Which of the following would demonstrate the essential skills required for this role? Tick the TWO correct answers.

	✓
The ability to work well as part of a team	
9 GCSE's including Grade B English and Mathematics	
Writing and delivering a presentation to 100 decision-makers	
3 years as Office Manager for a construction company	
AAT qualified	
A clean UK driving licence	

(b) Which THREE of the following would be the most relevant pieces of information to include in an application for this role?

	✓
5 years working as a Warehouse Manager	
A proven track record of excellent staff satisfaction	
Previous experience of working with an IT contractor	
A degree in Travel and Tourism Studies	
Achieving the best sales as an advisor in a clothes shop	
Putting new administrative systems in place in previous roles	
Playing football as part of a team every week-end	

(c) Which TWO of the following statements suggest that the candidate has the correct personal qualities for the role?

	✓
They are loyal and dedicated to the company they work for	
They believe that the system in place is usually the best one	
They like consulting with other staff to make decisions	
They write superb e-mails to colleagues and clients	
They often find errors in written and statistical reports	

(d) Which ONE of these candidates seems the best fit for the role?

	✓
Godfrey, formerly a History Professor with lots of qualifications, both academic and commercial. He has managed his own business but is a poor communicator.	
Erica, an experienced office worker, who has never managed staff and has had four jobs in the last year. She has superior organisational skills and loves to be part of a team.	
Mike, an experienced Office Manager, who likes to maintain current systems and prefers to take a more general view rather than looking into matters in detail.	
Rhea, an H.R. specialist, who has managed teams of office-based staff in the past. She has experience of developing processes and is used to communicating with clients.	

KAPLAN PUBLISHING

Test your understanding 3

The following statements come from a person specification in a job advertisement. Tick the boxes to show how each requirement is best described.

	Skill	Personal qualities	Experience	Qualifications
A background working in manufacturing				
An excellent verbal communicator				
Natural enthusiasm and dedication				
A university degree or similar				

 Test your understanding 4

Caroline is looking for a new job. The following personal qualities have been listed as desirable for the role: flexibility, courtesy and using initiative. She considers her recent experience and finds an example of each. Match the statement with the correct personal skill from the pick list provided.

In Caroline's first job, working for an online retailer in an administration role, she sometimes helped the credit control team to chase debts and the despatch team to pack orders.	
Caroline recently worked in a customer service role. She was often shouted at by angry customers, but always remained professional and respectful on the calls. She helped her colleagues when they experienced the same issues.	
In the customer service role, Caroline realised that many of the angry customers had not been provided with adequate tracking information. She therefore suggested a new online process to her team leader.	

Pick list

Flexibility   Courtesy   Using initiative

Case study

Jessica studied the skills list and realised that her avid interest in mathematics and her enjoyment of working with computers made **accountancy** the most favoured employment option for her.

She had also noticed that all organisations had one thing in common; they all need someone to keep their financial side of the business in order.

Having made her choice of career, Jessica set about looking for a suitable job vacancy.

2 Applying for a job

2.1 Creating a Curriculum Vitae (C.V.)

Before applying for a job, you will need to create a Curriculum Vitae, better known as a C.V.

 Definition

Curriculum Vitae is a Latin term meaning 'the course of a person's life'. It is a brief account of an individual's education, qualifications and previous occupations / career history. As such, it is typically a crucial part of any job application.

Your C.V. is therefore a document providing your personal details (such as address and contact information), as well as your educational background, examination results, previous employment and interests/hobbies. Where possible, it is also advisable to include your reasons for applying for the vacancy – this is often provided through a personal statement.

A C.V is the opportunity to introduce and sell yourself to a potential employer and make them want to select you for an interview and an opportunity to meet you in person.

In the USA and some other countries, C.V.s are often referred to as 'resumes'.

Typical sections on a C.V. include:

- **Personal Statement** – an overview of the individual's current situation, including a brief of summary of their past educational and professional background and an indication of their plans for the future. This section typically mentions key skills and/or industry sectors and can easily be adapted to make reference to an area of expertise mentioned in the job advertisement if required.

- **Education** – a listing of all qualifications achieved at school, college and university. This section of the C.V. is typically first to allow for the C.V. to run in chronological order (i.e. the earliest details first). However, as a considerable work history is established, it may be included in the lower part of the C.V., as the work experience gained may be deemed more important.

- **Employment / Work History** – usually detailing the most recent or current position first, this section lists all the individual's jobs. As a minimum, the job title, company name and dates are provided.

- **Experience** – can be easily merged with the Employment History and typically expands upon each role listed to describe key duties and responsibilities. This can be either in a list or written format, depending on individual preference. Sometimes a reason for leaving is included, although typically only where the employment was relatively short.

- **Key skills / Competencies** – this section gives an opportunity for to summarise the skills (whether professional or personal) which are considered most important. This section can be at the start of end of the C.V. Normally where the individual has little work experience, as will be the case for many people applying for jobs straight from full-time education, this section would not necessarily be relevant.

- **Hobbies and interests** – although some candidates are reluctant to put much detail in this section of the C.V., it helps employers to establish a picture of what the individual is like and evidence some of the personal qualities set out in the specification – for example, involvement in team sports would suggest a good team player; acting as a hobby would suggest the person is outgoing and a good verbal communicator.

- **References** – if successful, it may be necessary for a candidate's credentials (their personal qualities and work history) to be confirmed, both by previous employers (an employment reference) and other people who know them well (a personal or character reference), but are not close friends or relatives. Often this will include confirming dates of employment, attendance and disciplinary records and a brief summary of the person's character and worth ethic. It is unusual to include the names of these people on the C.V, typically stating that their details can be obtained 'on request'.

Case study

Jessica updated her C.V. ready to start applying for jobs:

Jessica Howard

Home Tel: 01234 567 89100
Mobile Tel: 07777 123456
E-mail: jessicahoward@website.co.uk

22 Any Street
Tweensville
Manchester M00 9LZ

Personal Profile

I have recently left full-time education. I am keen to study accountancy through work-based experience. I have good inter-personal skills giving me the ability to be an effective member of a team.

Quality is important to me; I believe that attention to detail should be focused on when completing any task. I am a reliable and flexible individual and I thrive on challenges. I take every opportunity to increase my skills and knowledge and actively seek ways to progress further.

Education

2012-2017
Farmer's School and Sixth Form Centre, Stockport, Cheshire SK99 0ZZ
GCSEs:

Subject	Grade Attained	Subject	Grade Attained
Mathematics	A*	Biology	B
English Literature	A	English Language	B
I.T.	A	Geography	C
History	C	French	C
Art	C		

Employment History

Oct 2014 – present
Shop Assistant, Howards Grocers, Manchester M95 6PV

Experience

Since the age of 14 years old, I have worked part–time in my uncle's grocery shop as a shop assistant, serving customers.

Due to showing an interest in the day to day running of the business, my uncle gave me a basic insight into VAT returns, paying wages and bookkeeping. However, he employed an accountant to ensure that all his finances were in order and up to date.

Hobbies and Interests

I play for a local netball team and enjoy all types of music, regularly going to concerts and festivals. I have recently started to volunteer in a local charity shop, where I serve customers and help to manage stock.

References

References available on request.

2.2   Personal information on a C.V.

Typically a C.V. will include the individual's name and primary contact details (address, e-mail and telephone numbers). These details are deemed necessary as a means of both contacting and identifying the individual (especially should they have a fairly common name).

Some people chose to also include a date of birth, photograph and/or other details, such as gender or marital status. These are by no means required as an employer should not make recruitment decisions (by law) based on a person's age, gender, marital status, race or religious/cultural background.

2.3   Application forms

An alternative to submitting a C.V. to apply for a job is to complete an application form. This can be either online or by filling a paper form. For some employers, they prefer both an application form and a C.V., while others ask for this instead of a C.V. This however remains quite uncommon in the private sector (although is more likely for public sector roles).

Application forms will ask for the same basic information as detailed on a C.V. but may ask specific questions relating to their organisation and the role that you are applying for. They may also ask why you think you are the most suitable candidate. Therefore the application form allows an employer to see how your experience and skills fit directly with the specific job specification, unlike a C.V. where this can be open to interpretation.

When completing an application form, research the company thoroughly before you fill it in, identify what relevant existing skills you have and what you can bring to the organisation. It is important to answer the actual questions being asked, as employers will compare different candidates' answers and therefore may be looking for relevant points.

When you have completed your C.V or an application form:

- check it to ensure your grammar and spelling are accurate.

- get someone to check the application form for you, they may be able to suggest additional information that you could include.

- ensure that you submit the application by the closing date otherwise it may not be considered.

2.4 Cover letters

Whether sending a C.V. or completing a form and whether online or on paper, it is important to include a cover letter or cover e-mail when applying for a role. This letter is designed primarily as an introduction to the application, an overview of the individual's suitability for the position and link key elements of the C.V. or form back to the original job specification.

It is important that the letter is not too long and focuses closely on why the applicant is a good match for the position. In this letter, unlike a C.V., reference will also be made to the organisation advertising the role and the desire to work for them.

Test your understanding 5

Consider the following statements regarding C.V.s and application forms. Tick the boxes to show if they are true or false.

Statement	True	False
A C.V. should always state your date of birth.		
A C.V. should always include details of your education.		
A C.V. should always include your previous employment history.		
On a C.V. you simply need to state the company and dates of your employment for each job.		
Every job application will require you supplying both an application form and your C.V.		
If you have a good C.V. there is no need to complete application forms when they are requested.		

3 Preparing for an interview

3.1 Interviews

If your application is successful and you are selected as a potential candidate for the role, you will be invited to attend an interview. They will state where the interview will take place, the date and time of the interview and who it is that will be interviewing you.

There are a number of different types of interview. The most common is a one-on-one, face-to-face interview with the recruiter. Typically this would be with the recruiting manager (likely to be the line manager of the possible future employer) and sometimes either another member of the department or a representative from the Human Resources (H.R.) department.

These types of interview tend to include a set of questions (followed for all applicants) which will focus on both the past experience of the candidate and the key skills required for the role. Although a role play or scenario is sometimes given to the interviewee to see how they would react in a real life situation, this would be more likely in a second interview, if one is seen to be necessary.

Other types of interview include:

- Panel interviews – where there are several representatives from the recruiting organisation judging the applicant

- Group interviews – where multiple candidates are given a set of tasks or questions to answer together (usually a limited number of them progress to another round of interviews)

- Assessment centres – similar to group interviews, but often involving a greater focus on competencies rather than the interaction between candidates

- Telephone / Skype interviews – in these cases, technology allows candidates to answer key questions without needing to attend in person.

3.2   Interview preparation

To succeed in a job interview, thorough preparation is key. The following tips are useful when preparing for an interview:

- Check the location and time of the interview and ensure you are not late – 10 - 15 minutes early is preferable.

- Get ready ahead of time - think about what you will wear, it is important to dress smartly in order to create a good first impression.

- Take any evidence of academic or professional qualifications with you.

- Practice your answers to any typical interview questions beforehand.

- Learn as much as you can about the organisation so that you are prepared for any questions that may be asked. This also shows that you are enthusiastic about gaining employment with them.

- Think of some questions that you may want to ask the employer.

- Try to find out who is interviewing you – this will enable for better practice when preparing and also for suitable answers.

- Read through the job advertisement and person specification in detail to ensure that you raise all of the key points.

- Read your C.V. or application form to make sure your answers are consistent.

3.3   Interview technique

It is equally important to make the right impression in an interview. Although it is important to be yourself and answer honestly, there may also be an element of performance required to impress recruiters on some occasions. Therefore it is important to:

- Speak clearly and give relevant, interesting answers.

- Listen carefully to anything the interviewer says and make reference to their questions and any information they give.

- Watch your body language - you want to appear confident throughout, regardless of how you may be feeling.

- Remain enthusiastic despite your nerves.

- Stay calm and professional.

Test your understanding 6

Which of the following would be considered to be good advice for a job interview? Tick the THREE most appropriate answers.

	✓
Think of some questions you would like to ask the interviewer	
Lie about your previous experience if it is necessary to get the job	
Ask the interviewer to read your CV rather than answering their questions in person	
Dress in smart casual clothes as you would if meeting your friends – it is important to be yourself	
Be enthusiastic and confident even if the situation makes you feel nervous	
Do not get to the interview too early – it can make recruiters less likely to be impressed if you seem too keen	
Research the organisation prior to the interview, including the company website and social media channels	

4 Summary and further questions

In this chapter we have looked at where to look for job vacancies and how to identify suitable jobs. You should now be able to distinguish between the different parts of job advertisements and provide examples of the skills and qualities required in person specifications, as well as being able to identify the skills and qualities deemed to be both 'essential' and 'desirable'.

In addition to this, you should be able to apply for a job, including the creation of a C.V. (or completion of an application form if necessary) and preparation for job interviews.

Let us return to our case study for further questions and to see how Jessica found and applied for a job. Her C.V. on page 38 will prove useful.

Case study

Jessica has seen a job vacancy for a Sales/Purchase Ledger junior with the following job description:

Sales/Purchase Ledger Junior

This is a great opportunity for someone looking to work for an expanding organisation and to start their career within accounting. AAT training will be offered to the successful candidate to help them progress within the business.

Salary £12,000 + monthly bonus + excellent benefits

Main Duties:

- Processing purchase ledger invoices
- Matching, batching and coding invoices
- Preparing payment runs
- Assisting with month-end procedures
- Coding and processing sales invoices
- Checking accuracy of invoices on Sage
- Reconciling customer & supplier accounts
- Chasing overdue payments from customers
- Recording receipts on Sage

Person Specification:

- GCSE Grades A-C in Maths and English
- Highly organised
- Great attention to detail
- A team player
- Friendly attitude and approach to others
- A knowledge of Office programs including Word and Excel

If you are interested in this role please download and complete the application form below and send it to Emma Snowdon at How Two Ltd. along with your CV before the 14th August 20X7.

Contact: emma@howtwoltd.co.uk

Case study activity 3

Using the job description provided, which of the following skills are essential (tick all that apply)?

	✓
Organisation	
Foreign language	
IT	
Problem solving	
Team working	

Which of the following personal qualities are required (tick all that apply)?

	✓
Friendly attitude	
Attention to detail	
Leadership qualities	
Using initiative	
Open to change	

Consider the following four statements regarding the experience and qualifications needed for this role. Are they true or false?

Statement	True	False
At least two years accounting experience is needed for this position.		
There is no requirement for considerable accounting experience for this position.		
No qualifications are needed for this role.		
The applicant needs to be AAT qualified.		

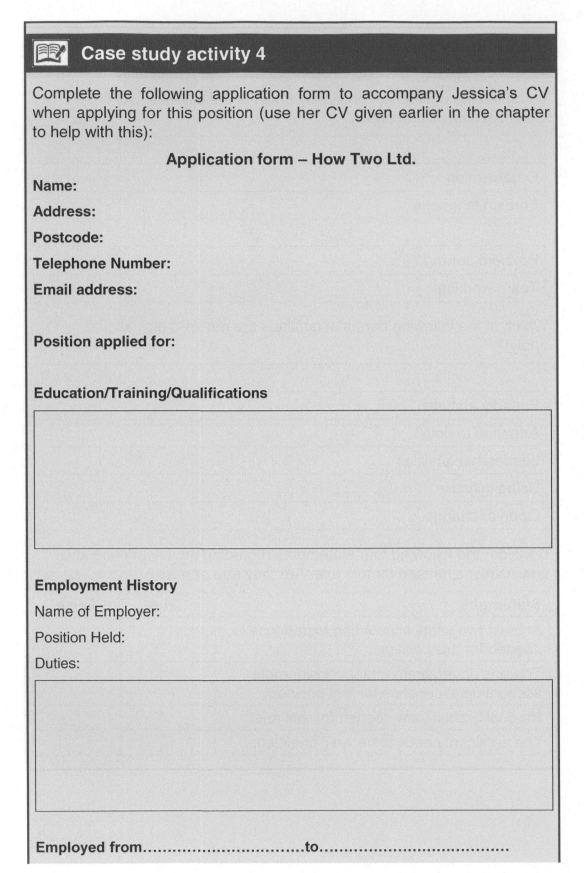

Case study activity 4

Complete the following application form to accompany Jessica's CV when applying for this position (use her CV given earlier in the chapter to help with this):

Application form – How Two Ltd.

Name:

Address:

Postcode:

Telephone Number:

Email address:

Position applied for:

Education/Training/Qualifications

Employment History

Name of Employer:

Position Held:

Duties:

Employed from...................................to...

Reason for leaving:

Please tell us why you applied for this position and why you think you are the best person for the job:

Please tell us if there are any dates when you will not be available for interview:

I can confirm that to the best of my knowledge the above information is correct. I accept that providing deliberately false information could result in my dismissal.

Signature .... Date ....

Case study activity 5

Jessica is preparing to attend an interview at How Two Ltd.

Which FOUR of the following would be appropriate behaviour for Jessica before and during the interview?

	✓
Checking the time and location of the interview	
Dressing in smart work attire for the interview	
Eating during the interview	
Using her research of the company to be critical of its management during the interview	
Telling the interviewer how keen she is to work for the company	
Checking for text messages of support on her mobile phone during the interview	
Calling the Managing Director 'James' after he introduced himself as Mr Gregory	
Asking the interviewer how long the interview will last after 15 minutes of questions	
Asking questions at the end of the interview about the training she will receive	

Answers to chapter activities

 Test your understanding 1

Example	Organisational	Written communication	Verbal communication	IT
Weekly e-mail bulletins to key clients		✓		
Booking an off-site meeting for managers	✓			
Creating a spreadsheet of all suppliers used by the company				✓
Doing a presentation on charity ideas to your department			✓	

 Test your understanding 2

(a)   Which of the following would demonstrate the essential skills required for this role? Tick the TWO correct answers.

	✓
The ability to work well as part of a team	
9 GCSE's including Grade B English and Mathematics	
Writing and delivering a presentation to 100 decision-makers	✓
3 years as Office Manager for a construction company	✓
AAT qualified	
A clean UK driving licence	

(b) Which THREE of the following would be the most relevant pieces of information to include in an application for this role?

	✓
5 years working as a Warehouse Manager	
A proven track record of excellent staff satisfaction	✓
Previous experience of working with an IT contractor	✓
A degree in Travel and Tourism Studies	
Achieving the best sales as an advisor in a clothes shop	
Putting new administrative systems in place in previous roles	✓
Playing football as part of a team every week-end	

(c) Which TWO of the following statements suggest that the candidate has the correct personal qualities for the role?

	✓
They are loyal and dedicated to the company they work for	✓
They believe that the system in place is usually the best one	
They like consulting with other staff to make decisions	
They write superb e-mails to colleagues and clients	
They often find errors in written and statistical reports	✓

(d) Which ONE of these candidates seems the best fit for the role?

	✓
Godfrey, formerly a History Professor with lots of qualifications, both academic and commercial. He has managed his own business but is a poor communicator.	
Erica, an experienced office worker, who has never managed staff and has had four jobs in the last year. She has superior organisational skills and loves to be part of a team.	
Mike, an experienced Office Manager, who likes to maintain current systems and prefers to take a more general view rather than looking into matters in detail.	
Rhea, an H.R. specialist, who has managed teams of office-based staff in the past. She has experience of developing processes and is used to communicating with clients.	✓

KAPLAN PUBLISHING

Test your understanding 3

	Skill	Personal qualities	Experience	Qualifications
A background working in manufacturing			✓	
An excellent verbal communicator	✓			
Natural enthusiasm and dedication		✓		
A university degree or similar				✓

Test your understanding 4

In Caroline's first job, working for an online retailer in an administration role, she sometimes helped the credit control team to chase debts and the despatch team to pack orders.	**Flexibility**
Caroline recently worked in a customer service role. She was often shouted at by angry customers, but always remained professional and respectful on the calls. She helped her colleagues when they experienced the same issues.	**Courtesy**
In the customer service role, Caroline realised that many of the angry customers had not been provided with adequate tracking information. She therefore suggested a new online process to her team leader.	**Using initiative**

Test your understanding 5

Statement	True	False
A C.V. should always state your date of birth.		✓
A C.V. should always include details of your education.	✓	
A C.V. should always include your previous employment history.	✓	
On a C.V. you simply need to state the company and dates of your employment for each job.		✓
Every job application will require you supplying both an application form and your C.V.		✓
If you have a good C.V. there is no need to complete application forms when they are requested.		✓

Test your understanding 6

	✓
Think of some questions you would like to ask the interviewer	✓
Lie about your previous experience if it is necessary to get the job	
Ask the interviewer to read your CV rather than answering their questions in person	
Dress in smart casual clothes as you would if meeting your friends – it is important to be yourself	
Be enthusiastic and confident even if the situation makes you feel nervous	✓
Do not get to the interview too early – it can make recruiters less likely to be impressed if you seem too keen	
Research the organisation prior to the interview, including the company website and social media channels	✓

Case study activity 3

Using the job description provided, which of the following skills are essential (tick all that apply)?

	✓
Organisation	✓
Foreign language	
IT	✓
Problem solving	
Team working	✓

Which of the following personal qualities are required (tick all that apply)?

	✓
Friendly attitude	✓
Attention to detail	✓
Leadership qualities	
Using initiative	
Open to change	

Consider the following four statements regarding the experience and qualifications needed for this role. Are they true or false?

Statement	True	False
At least two years accounting experience is needed for this position.		✓
There is no requirement for considerable accounting experience for this position.	✓	
No qualifications are needed for this role.		✓
The applicant needs to be AAT qualified.		✓

Case study activity 4

Application form – How Two Ltd.

Name: Jessica Howard

Address: 22 Any Street, Tweensville, Manchester

Postcode: M00 9LZ

Telephone Number: 07777 123456 / 01234 567 89100

Email address: jessicahoward@website.co.uk

Position applied for: Sales and Purchase Ledger Junior

Education/Training/Qualifications

2012-2017: Farmer's School and Sixth Form Centre, Stockport, Cheshire SK99 0ZZ			
GSCE's:			
Mathematics	A*	Biology	B
English	A	English	B
Literature	A	Language	C
I.T.	C	Geography	C
History	C	French	
Art			

Employment History

Name of Employer: Howards Grocers, Manchester M95 6PV

Position Held: Shop Assistant

Duties:

- Serving customers / cashier
- Stocking shelves
- Assisted with stock taking
- Got an insight to how the financial aspect of owning a shop works

Employed from October 2014 **to** Present

Reason for leaving:

Currently still employed on a part-time basis, having worked there during education. I will only leave when I have secured permanent employment with a career pathway. This is a family business, belonging to my uncle and therefore I do not have to give notice.

Please tell us why you applied for this position and why you think you are the best person for the job:

I enjoy mathematics (this was my favourite subject at school) and I have a natural flair for numbers and problem-solving. I feel that this combined with my initial knowledge of finances from my uncle's business will serve me well for this role. I also enjoy Information Technology and am competent in the use of all Office programs.

I am a keen and willing student and I pay attention to detail with any task that I am given. I am an honest and reliable individual, with excellent communication skills. I am also a good team player, as shown by my membership of a netball team.

I believe that my existing skills, qualifications and avid interest in your company's products make me an ideal candidate for the job.

Please tell us if there are any dates when you will not be available for interview:

None

I can confirm that to the best of my knowledge the above information is correct. I accept that providing deliberately false information could result in my dismissal.

Signature   *Jessica Howard*   **Date**   *1ˢᵗ August 20X7*

Case study activity 5

Which FOUR of the following would be appropriate behaviour for Jessica before and during the interview?

	✓
Checking the time and location of the interview	✓
Dressing in smart work attire for the interview	✓
Eating during the interview	
Using her research of the company to be critical of its management during the interview	
Telling the interviewer how keen she is to work for the company	✓
Checking for text messages of support on her mobile phone during the interview	
Calling the Managing Director 'James' after he introduced himself as Mr Gregory	
Asking the interviewer how long the interview will last after 15 minutes of questions	
Asking questions at the end of the interview about the training she will receive	✓

Using numbers in business

Introduction

When you are working in an accounting department you will need to be confident in handling money and working with numbers. You will also be expected to be able to use a calculator effectively

This chapter covers the essential mathematical skills you will need to perform common accounting calculations: addition and subtraction, multiplication and division, percentages, ratios and fractions, and calculating the average of a range of numbers.

KNOWLEDGE	CONTENTS
Using numbers in business	1 Mathematic symbols
1.1 Record and sort whole numbers	2 Decimal places and rounding up and down
2.1 Check results of calculations	3 Addition and subtraction
2.2 Identify differences between figures over time	4 Multiplication and division
2.3 Complete calculations	5 Fractions and ratios
3.1 Calculate decimals, fractions and percentages of numbers	6 Percentages
	7 Calculating Averages
3.2 Calculate equivalent fractions, percentages and decimals	8 Identifying differences and checking results of calculations
3.3 Calculate and apply simple proportions and ratios	9 Summary and Interview Assessment
3.4 Round numbers	

1 Mathematic symbols

1.1 Case study: an introduction

 Case study

Jessica was very excited to be invited for an interview. As part of the interview process she was informed that she would have to complete a mathematics assessment, she was given a brief overview of what would be covered.

Even though Jessica was a grade A* student and the assessment sounded easy to her, the prospect of completing it made her really nervous so she decided to undertake some revision.

1.2 Common symbols

The following table shows the most common symbols you will see for the mathematical functions you will be using in this unit.

	Addition	Subtraction	Multiplication	Division
Calculator	+	-	X	÷
Computer keyboard	+	-	*	/
Written	+	- or ( )	X or @	$\frac{2}{3}$

 Case study

As part of the interview assessment Jessica needs to know how to use the different numerical functions.

Using the figures 8 and 4, the following calculations would be performed:

	Addition	Subtraction	Multiplication	Division
Calculator	8 + 4	8 - 4	8 x 4	8 ÷ 4
Computer keyboard	8 + 4	8 - 4	8 * 4	8 / 4
Written	8 + 4	8 - 4	8 x 4	8 ÷ 4
Answer	**12**	**4**	**32**	**2**

1.3 Punctuation

In the UK a full stop [.] is used to separate pounds and pence and a comma [,] is used to separate thousands. For example, to make it easier to see the difference between £1000000, £100000 and £10000 count 3 zeros back from the right and put a comma, then count another 3 zeros back from the first comma and put another comma, and so on.

- £1000000 becomes £1,000,000 or one million pounds
- £100000 becomes £100,000 or one hundred thousand pounds
- £10000 becomes £10,000 or ten thousand pounds.

When you are dealing with a long list of numbers putting the commas in the right place makes the figures easier to read, and you will be able to perform the calculations more efficiently.

Note: Some countries use commas for the decimal point and the thousand separator is shown by a full stop. Always follow the convention of the country you are working in.

1.4 Currency

For numbers that represent money you should always show the relevant currency symbol. The currency symbol for UK sterling pounds is £. Euros are represented by €, and for US dollars the symbol is $. You can either write the symbol against each amount or the currency symbol can be shown at the top of the list.

 Case study

How Two Ltd. is a multinational organisation, meaning that they have offices in several countries. As a result, they deal with currency in different forms including pounds, euros and US dollars.

As part of the interview assessment, Jessica needs to know how work with common units of currency. This will be important if dealing with Sales and Purchases from different countries.

The sales from last week are listed below:

	UK Sales	European Sales	American Sales
Monday	565484	235987	456987
Tuesday	897342	342565	432664
Wednesday	1018765	287900	473990
Thursday	542890	401389	489014
Friday	675989	307999	455555

Required:

Add up the sales for each country; make the figures easier to read and use the appropriate currency symbol for the totals.

Case study

Solution:

	UK Sales		European Sales		American Sales	
Monday	565484	**565,484**	235987	**235,987**	456987	**456,987**
Tuesday	897342	**897,342**	342565	**342,565**	432664	**432,664**
Wednesday	1018765	**1,018,765**	287900	**287,900**	473990	**473,990**
Thursday	542890	**542,890**	401389	**401,389**	489014	**489,014**
Friday	675989	**675,989**	307999	**307,999**	455555	**455,555**
Total	**£3,700,470**		**€1,575,840**		**$2,308,210**	

Written in words:

UK Sales – Three million, seven hundred thousand, four hundred and seventy pounds.

European Sales – One million, five hundred and seventy-five thousand, eight hundred and forty euros.

American Sales – Two million, three hundred and eight thousand, two hundred and ten dollars.

2 Decimal places and rounding up and down

2.1 Decimal places

For the AAT assessment, the instructions will always tell you whether you should round your answer to the nearest pound (whole number), or to one or two decimal places.

Whole number: £500 Five hundred pounds

Two decimal places: £49.99 Forty nine pounds and ninety nine pence

One decimal place: £2.5 million Two and a half million pounds

Note: If you are using a calculator the display will not show the second decimal point if it is zero. When writing the answer down you should always include the missing zero.

Case study

The job role that Jessica is applying for includes working with both sales and purchases. This means that Jessica must be able to round figures accurately when generating sales invoices or when checking purchase invoices.

When calculating amounts to be entered on a sales invoice, the following steps should be taken:

A customer buys 5 items costing £2.50 each. You enter 5 times £2.50 by keying 5 x 2.50 on the calculator. The display shows 12.5.

			5 x 2.50 =
			12.5
(	)	%	AC
7	8	9	÷
4	5	6	×
1	2	3	−
0	.	=	+

This answer should be written as £12.50 to show the pounds and pence.

In the workplace, always check how many decimal places you should show. If you are not sure, show your answers to two decimal places.

Monetary amounts should always be shown to one or two decimal places, or whole numbers. However, the calculator may show more figures after the decimal place than you need, so you will need to round your answer.

2.2   Showing pounds and pence to two decimal places

Calculations which require the answer to be shown in pounds and pence should always be given to two decimal places. If your calculator shows more than two decimal places, you will need to round the answer.

Look at the number in the third decimal place – if it is 5 or above, round the number in the second decimal place up. If it is below 5, the answer is rounded down – you do not need to change the number in the second decimal place.

2.3 Rounding up

 Case study

Jessica may also be asked to calculate the cost of a single item when a number of items have been charged for. The following steps should be taken:

If you are asked, for example, to calculate the cost of one box of a product when 3 boxes cost £500, you do the following:

- divide £500.00 by 3 by keying 500. ÷ 3 on the calculator.

The display shows 166.666666667.

As the third decimal place is larger than 5, you should round this answer **up** to the nearest penny - £166.67.

2.4 Rounding down

 Case study

Jessica may also be asked to calculate the cost of a single item when a number of items have been charged for. The following steps should be taken:

If you are told, for example, that a supplier has given you a price of £100.00 for 3 boxes of a product and you need to know the cost for one box you do the following:

- divide £100.00 by 3 by keying 100. ÷ 3 on the calculator.

The display shows 33.3333333333

As the third decimal place is below 5, this answer should be rounded **down** to the nearest penny. This means you do not have to change the figure in the second decimal place, so the answer is £33.33.

2.5   Rounding answers to the nearest whole number

To round numbers to the nearest whole number, you need to look at the number in the first decimal place - if the number in the first decimal place is 5 or above, round up the pounds figure. If it is below 5, round down the pounds figure – you do not need to change the pounds figure.

Example

You have been asked to round the following figures to the nearest whole pound.

Original figure	Rounded to the nearest whole pound	Notes
£49.99	£50	The number in the first decimal place is 9 – the pounds figure is rounded up.
£425.20	£425	The number in the first decimal place is 2 – the pounds figure is rounded down. You do not need to change the pounds figure.

3 Addition and subtraction

3.1 Addition and subtraction in accounting

There are many tasks in the accounting function where you will be required to add and subtract lists of numbers. You will need to complete these tasks confidently and efficiently. You should always add up lists of numbers twice to check that you get the same answer both times.

When you are writing down lists of numbers make sure that the decimal points are aligned, so that the figures are easier to read and calculate.

 Example - addition

You have been asked to add the weekly sales and you have written the following list.

Monday	£15,000.00
Tuesday	£14,500.50
Wednesday	£ 9,250.00
Thursday	£16,700.00
Friday	£18,000.00
Saturday	£25,000.00

Using a calculator effectively

When working with monetary numbers you should always key in the decimal point on the calculator. If you need to add a whole number you do not need to key in the zeros after the decimal place and if the pence are a multiple of 10 you do not need to key in the final zero.

Use this technique to add up the list of weekly sales.

The answer on your calculator will be:

15000. + 14500.5 + 9250. + 16700. + 18000. + 25000. =

98450.5

This answer should be written down as **£98,450.50**

Test your understanding 1

The Sales department have been given the following information for last week's sales.

Credit Sales	Monday	£ 22,399.00
	Tuesday	£ 23,210.50
	Wednesday	£ 22,225.20
	Thursday	£ 24,375.00
	Friday	£ 16,010.00

Cash Sales	Monday	£ 2,499.99
	Tuesday	£ 3,325.50
	Wednesday	£ 2,769.00
	Thursday	£ 2,005.00
	Friday	£ 2,247.20

You have been asked to:

a)   Calculate the weekly credit sales

b)   Calculate the weekly cash sales

c)   Calculate the total weekly sales

 Definitions

Sales – the exchange of goods or services to an individual or organisation in exchange for money.

Cash sales – sales made where a payment is taken at the point of sale (immediately on the supply of the goods). The payment itself can be made by cash (currency), cheque, debit or credit card, or bank transfer. An example of a cash sale is when you go into a shop, choose the items you want to buy, and pay in the shop.

Credit sales – sales made where the goods or services will be paid later than the point of sale. Many organisations give credit to their regular trade customers so that one payment can be made for all the transactions made in each month.

3.2 Subtraction to calculate profit

As stated in Chapter 1, all private sector organisations' primary purpose is to make profit. Therefore it is important to know how to calculate the profit (or loss) a business has made.

Profit is the amount of money an organisation earns after expenditure has been deducted from income. If an organisation spends more money than it has earned, this is known as a loss. This will be covered in depth in Chapter 6.

 Definition

Cost of Sales – The direct cost of producing the goods and services that have been sold.

Gross profit – The profit (or amount of money left) from sales after the cost of sales has been deducted.

Net profit – The amount left from sales income (gross profit) after cost of sales and all other expenses (such as wages, electricity and marketing costs) have been deducted.

To calculate gross profit, cost of sales are subtracted from sales income.

To calculate net profit, all other expenditure is subtracted from gross profit.

Although for your assessment it is not necessary to distinguish between gross and net profit, the following examples show how both are calculated as both terms are widely used and both types of profit are calculated in business.

Case study

How Two Ltd's sales income for the last month has been calculated to be £98,000.

The cost of sales came to £58,800 and other expenditure was £25,000.

Jessica is to calculate the gross profit and the net profit.

a) Calculate gross profit

She should:

Subtract the cost of sales, £58,800 from the sales income, £98,000.

To do so, key in 98000 – 58000 =

Therefore, the gross profit is £39,200.

b) Calculate net profit

Jessica should:

Subtract all other expenditure, £25,000 from the gross profit, £39,200.

To do so, key in 39200 – 25000 =

Therefore, the net profit is £14,200.

Example

You have been given the following financial information for a business:

Sales income	£259,258.75
Cost of sales	£156,540.00
Wages	£85,000.00
Marketing	£5,297.50
Premises costs	£3,200.00
Vehicle costs	£2,785.80

Required:

Calculate:

a) Gross profit

b) Net profit

Solution

a) To calculate gross profit, subtract £156,540.00 from £259,258.75

259258.75 - 156540. =

102718.75

Gross profit is £102,718.75

b) There are two methods for calculating net profit:

i. Subtract each expense from the gross profit figure:

102718.75 - 85000. - 5297.5 - 3200. - 2785.80 =

6435.45

Net profit is £6,435.45

ii. First add up all the other expenditure, and then subtract that figure from your gross profit figure of £102,748.75

85000. + 5297.50 + 3200. + 2785.80 =

96283.3

102718.75 - 96283.3 =

6435.45

Net profit is £6,435.45

 Test your understanding 2

For October, How Two Ltd. had credit sales of £258,956.50 and cash sales of £25,985.60.

The cost of sales figure was £155,215.35

Other expenses were:

Wages	£ 65,500.00
Advertising	£ 12,576.00
Heat and light	£ 10,040.50
Administration	£ 12,875.70
Vehicle costs	£ 4,950.75

Calculate:

a)   The total sales income

b)   Gross profit

c)   Net profit

---

4   Multiplication and division

4.1   Multiplying in accounting

Many calculations that you perform in an accounting office will require you to multiply or divide.

 Definition

Multiplying means adding the same amount a number of times. If you need to find the cost of more than one item you multiply the cost of the item by the number of items needed.

Multiplying a number by another will **increase** the original amount.

Case study

A customer of How Two Ltd has bought the following goods and has asked you to calculate the total sales price.

- 5   AG 355 15" laptop computer @ £299.00
- 3 Tamsing 10" Tablet PC @ £199.00
- 8 Shogun USB External Hard Drive @ £50.00
- 1 Tiger Antivirus Pro (10 licenses) @ £29.99

Setting the information out clearly in a table will help you to calculate the prices efficiently and will look more professional.

Item	Quantity	Unit Price (£)	Total Price (£)	Calculation
AG 355 15" laptop computer	5	299.00	**1,495.00**	*5 x 299*
Tamsing 10" Tablet PC	3	199.00	**597.00**	*3 x 199*
Shogun USB External Hard Drive	8	50.00	**400.00**	*8 x 50*
Tiger Antivirus Pro (10 licenses)	1	29.99	**29.99**	*1 x 29.99*
Total Sales Price			**2,521.99**	*1495.00+ 597.00+ 400.00 +29.99*

4.2 Division in accounting

Definition

Dividing a number means splitting it into parts. If you know the cost of a number of items and want to find the cost of just one of them you will use division.

Dividing a number by another will **decrease** the original amount.

KAPLAN PUBLISHING

Case study

The How Two customer has seen some mouse mats for sale at £12.50 for a pack of 5. The customer would like to know the cost for each mouse mat.

To calculate the cost per unit, divide the total cost by the number of units

Total cost per pack of mouse mats is £12.50

Divided by the number of units 5

Calculation:

12.5 ÷ 5 =

2.5

Each individual mouse mat costs **£2.50**

The same principles as those above for calculating prices could also be used for a variety of key daily routines of an accounting department. Let us consider the payroll function to test how multiplication and division are useful.

 Test your understanding 3

You have been asked to calculate the weekly gross pay for the following employees.

Gross pay is the total amount of money paid to an employee before taxes or other deductions are made.

- Kamal worked for 35 hours and is paid £7.20 per hour.
- Pamela worked for 35 hours and is paid £8.50 per hour.
- Jason worked for 16 hours and is paid £8.50 per hour.
- Sana worked for 8 hours and is paid £7.20 per hour.

Required:

Set the information out in a table and calculate

a) The gross pay for each employee
b) The total gross pay for all employees.

Test your understanding 4

You have been given the following information from the previous payroll.

Kamal is paid £7.20 per hour. Last week Kamal earned £216.00.

Calculate how many hours Kamal worked last week.

5 Fractions and ratios

5.1 Using fractions

 Definition

Fractions are another way of representing parts of whole numbers.

If something is shared out equally between two people, each receives a half of the total, and that is written as $\frac{1}{2}$

The top half of a fraction is the **numerator.** The bottom half of a fraction is the **denominator.**

The numerator is divided by the denominator to show the decimal form of the fraction.

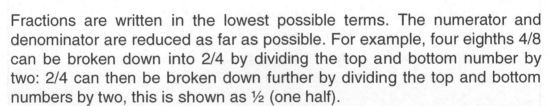

$$\frac{1}{2} = 1 \div 2 = 0.5$$

Fractions are written in the lowest possible terms. The numerator and denominator are reduced as far as possible. For example, four eighths 4/8 can be broken down into 2/4 by dividing the top and bottom number by two: 2/4 can then be broken down further by dividing the top and bottom numbers by two, this is shown as ½ (one half).

Remember! Whatever you do to the top number, you must do the same to the bottom number when trying to break a fraction down into its lowest form.

Large fractions can be reduced by dividing both the denominator and the numerator by the largest number that goes into both exactly.

For example, each number in the fraction 18/54 can be divided by 18 so, the fraction is reduced to:

$$\frac{18 \div 18 \;=\; 1}{54 \div 18 \;=\; 3} \quad \text{or one third}$$

 Case study

As part of her assessment, Jessica must be able to demonstrate that she can calculate simple fractions and then convert them into decimals:

Breaking the fractions down into their lowest form:

a)   50/100 (divide both numbers by 10) = 5/10 (divide both numbers by 5) = ½

b)   4/16 (divide both numbers by 2) = 2/8 (divide both numbers by 2) = ¼

c)   30/150 (divide both numbers by 5) = 6/30 (divide both numbers by 6) = 1/5

d)   20/200 (divide both numbers by 10) = 2/20 (divide both numbers by 2) = 1/10

Note: It doesn't matter what number you divide by so long as it goes into both the top and bottom number equally.

Jessica must then be able to convert fractions into decimals:

Converting the above fractions into decimals:

a)   ½ = 1 ÷ 2 = 0.5

b)   ¼ = 1 ÷ 4 = 0.25

c)   1/5 = 1 ÷ 5 = 0.2

d)   1/10 = 1 ÷ 10 = 0.1

5.2   Calculating a given fraction of a whole number

To calculate the fraction of a whole number:

- divide the whole number by the denominator (the bottom number)

- multiply the answer by the numerator (the top number).

Example

Bennett & Sons produce and sell home appliances, including electrical equipment for domestic use. The company has four branches in the UK: South Park, North Park, East Park and West Park.

The total sales income for all branches was £2,700,000.

North Park made $\frac{2}{3}$ of the sales.

How much sales income did North Park make?

1. Divide the total sales income by the denominator (the bottom number).

$$\frac{£2,700,000}{3} = £900,000$$

2. Multiply the £900,000 by the numerator (the top number).

$$2 \times £900,000 = £1,800,000$$

The calculation can be written as:

$$\frac{£2,700,000}{3} \times 2$$

North Park made £1,800,000 worth of sales.

Tip:

To use your calculator efficiently leave the zeros out of your calculation:

$$\frac{27}{3} \times 2 = 18$$

Just remember to add back the zeros you didn't calculate: 1800000 and to include the currency sign and thousand separators. £1,800,000.

 Test your understanding 5

How Two Ltd manufactures mouse mats in three different colours: blue, black and red. The production manager has estimated that 540,000 mouse mats will be produced next month and $\frac{3}{5}$ will be black.

How many black mouse mats will be produced?

Test your understanding 6

How Two Ltd has 45,000 customers at one of their branches. $\frac{2}{3}$ of these customers pay on credit.

How many of the customers are cash customers?

 Test your understanding 7

The Director of How Two Ltd has organised a meal in a restaurant for three of the managers and their families as a reward for their hard work over the last month.

The Morris family consists of two adults and three children.

The Kazee family consists of two adults and two children.

The Thomas family consist of one adult and one child.

The restaurant bill totals £210.56. How can the bill be split so that each family pays a fair proportion of the £210.56?

5.3 Expressing a number as a fraction of another number

When expressing a number as a fraction of another number you simply use the smaller number as the numerator (the top number) and the bigger number as the denominator (the bottom number).

You then break the fraction down into its lowest form.

 Example

Bennett & Sons made the following sales of kitchen appliances in one week at their North Park branch:

Day	Number of kitchen appliances sold
Monday	20
Tuesday	40
Wednesday	50
Thursday	10
Friday	60
Total	**180**

To express the number of kettles sold each day as a fraction of the total number sold during the week:

Monday	20/180 = 2/18 = 1/9
Tuesday	40/180 = 4/18 = 2/9
Wednesday	50/180 = 5/18
Thursday	10/180 = 1/18
Friday	60/180 = 6/18 = 1/3

Note: You can check your answer by doing the following:

Monday	180 ÷ 9 x 1 = 20
Tuesday	180 ÷ 9 x 2 = 40
Wednesday	180 ÷ 18 x 5 = 50
Thursday	180 ÷ 18 x 1 = 10
Friday	180 ÷ 3 x 1 = 60

5.4 Ratios

Ratios give exactly the same information as fractions but they are written in a different way so that comparisons can be made between two numbers.

They are a way of comparing amounts of something. For example, if there were 15 men and 12 women in the Sales department, this would be expressed as 15:12 *'fifteen to twelve'*.

This could be broken down into its lowest form the same way as a fraction could (by dividing both numbers by the same number):

15 ÷ 3 = 5

12 ÷ 3 = 4

This would be written as 5:4; *pronounced 'five to four'*.

5 : 4

The two numbers given in a ratio are the fraction numerators.

The denominator is not shown - it can be calculated by adding together the two numerators

In this ratio, 3 and 1 are the fraction numerators.

The denominator is 4.

3 : 1

This ratio is pronounced 'three to one'.

Case study

How Two Ltd are reviewing two of their retail outlets with total sales of £56,000.

The pattern of sales for Store A and Store B has been given as ratio of 3:1 respectively. This means that Store A has 3 *times* more sales than Store B.

To calculate the ratio the two numerators are added together to find the denominator: 3 + 1 = 4.

We can then apportion the total sales of £56,000 between to the two retail outlets as follows:

Store A $\dfrac{56,000}{4}$ x 3 = £42,000

Store B $\dfrac{56,000}{4}$ x 1 = 14 = £14,000

You may be asked to calculate the ratio or proportion of two given numbers. Let's use the numbers from the two stores above.

 Case study

Store A has sales of £42,000 and Store B has sales of £14,000. This time you have been asked to find out the ratio of Store A's sales to Store B's.

First, divide   Store A's sales $\dfrac{£42,000}{£14,000} = 3$

By   Store B's sales

We are comparing Store A to Store B, so the ratio answer is written as 3:1.

 Test your understanding 8

How Two Ltd has two departments who use the canteen at their headquarters. There are 125 employees in the production department and 25 employees in the administration department.

What is the ratio of production department employees to administration staff?

Test your understanding 9

Bennett & Son's West Park branch has cost of sales of £75,000 and sales of £250,000.

What is the ratio of cost of sales to sales?

6 Percentages

6.1 The use of percentages

Percentages are another method used to compare figures. 'Per cent' means 'out of a 100' so the denominator of the percentage is 100.

Percentages can be shown as fractions or decimals:

$25\% = \dfrac{25}{100} = 0.25$

$10\% = \dfrac{10}{100} = 0.10$

Tip: It is more efficient to calculate percentages on a calculator by using the decimal equivalent.

 Test your understanding 10

Use your calculator to fill in the missing figures from the table below.

Percentage	Fraction	Decimal
25%	$\dfrac{25}{100}$	
	$\dfrac{2}{100}$	0.02
10%		0.10
1%	$\dfrac{1}{100}$	
50%		0.50
	$\dfrac{5}{100}$	0.05

KAPLAN PUBLISHING

6.2   Finding a percentage of a whole number

 Case study

Jessica will need to be able to find a percentage of a whole number, for example when calculating how much discount to deduct from a sales invoice, or when adding VAT on to an invoice.

 Definition

VAT (Value Added Tax) is a government tax on some consumer goods. Organisations that are registered for VAT must collect this tax from customers on behalf of the government. In 2017 the VAT rate was 20%.

To calculate percentages efficiently on a calculator, you must first convert the percentage to a decimal; you can then use this figure in your calculation.

We will now look at two examples to illustrate this method – the first shows how to find a percentage from a total value (in this case, of sales) and the second relates the same method to VAT.

 Example

Bennett & Sons has four branches in the UK: South Park, North Park, East Park and West Park.

North Park had Month 1 sales of £24,560.

The total sales to date for all branches was £122,800.

To express North Park's Month 1 sales as a percentage of the total sales:

24,560 ÷ 122,800 = 0.2

x 100 = 20%

North Park's Month 1 sales as a percentage of total sales = 20%

Note: You can check your answer by doing:

122,800 ÷100 x 20 = 24,560

Example

A customer (Pipers Plumbers) has bought a monitor worth £150.00 from How Two Ltd and has been offered 10% discount.

VAT of 20% is to be added to the invoice amount.

You are to calculate the total amount the customer owes.

Discount

- Convert 10% to a decimal: $10\% = \dfrac{10}{100} = 0.10$

- Multiply £150.00 by 0.10 = £15.00 discount

- **Subtract** £15.00 from £150.00 to find the net amount = £135.00

VAT

- Convert 20% to a decimal: $20\% = \dfrac{20}{100} = 0.20$

- Multiply the net amount of £135.00 by 0.20 = £27.00 VAT

- **Add** £27.00 to £135.00 to find the total amount = £162.00

These calculations are shown on the following invoice:

How Two Ltd	
VAT NO. 456 7656 909	
Pipers Plumbers Bolton Close Rochdale FG1 3SQ	Invoice no: i459009 Tax point: 24 May 2017
Monitor	£150.00
Less Discount 10%	-£15.00
Total after discount	£135.00
VAT at 20%	£27.00
Total	£162.00
Payment terms: 15 days net	

Test your understanding 11

Complete the following invoices.

How Two Ltd

VAT NO. 456 7656 909

Grange Theatre
Blackburn Avenue
Diggle
LF2 689

Invoice no: 5678
Tax point: 23 September 2017

HDMI Cable	£75.00
Less Discount 5%	£
Total after discount	£
VAT at 20%	£
Total	£

Payment terms: 7 days net

How Two Ltd

VAT NO. 456 7656 909

H Kazee
Bristol Street
Gloucester
AL9 867

Invoice no: 35281
Tax point: 26 September 2017

5 x HB78 @ £15.00	£
10 x AN5787 @ £2.30	£
Sub total	£
Less 15% discount	£
Total after discount	£
VAT at 20%	
Total	£

Payment terms: 7 days net

6.3 Calculating the percentage of one number in relation to another

 Example

The East Park branch of Bennett & Sons has sales of £890,000 and gross profit of £267,000. We need to calculate gross profit as a percentage of sales.

Divide gross profit
Into sales
$$\frac{£267,000}{£890,000} = 0.30 \text{ then multiply by } 100 = 30\%$$

Gross profit is 30% of sales.

Check your answer by multiplying sales of £890,000 by 0.30 = £267,000.

Test your understanding 12

The human resources department has analysed the number of employees at one of How Two's regional offices.

	No of employees	Percentage of the total number of employees
Production department	8	
Marketing department	3	
Accounts department	2	
Sales department	4	
Total number of employees	17	

Calculate the number of employees in each department as a percentage of the total number of employees. Round your answers to one decimal place.

7 Calculating averages

7.1 Calculating the range

 Case study

As part of the job role at How Two Ltd., Jessica must be able to calculate the range of a set of figures.

The range is the difference between the highest and lowest figure in a set of data.

 Case study

How Two Ltd have collated information on the number of hours worked by the admin staff in their main office over a week.

Adam – 35 hours

Steph – 38 hours

John – 42 hours

Maisie – 45 hours

Jim – 30 hours

Step One: Put them in order to make it easier to see the highest and the lowest.

30, 35, 38, 42, 45

The highest number is 45 and the lowest number is 30.

Step Two: Find the difference by subtracting the lower number from the highest number.

45 – 30 = 15

The range is 15.

7.2 Identifying the mode

 Case study

As part of the job role at How Two Ltd., Jessica must be able to identify the most frequently occurring number in a set of numbers (**the mode**).

To find the mode, or modal value, first put the numbers in order, then count how many of each number there are. The number that appears the most often is the mode.

Note: It doesn't matter whether you list the numbers in ascending order (smallest to biggest) or in descending order (biggest to smallest), it's simply the number that appears the most.

 Case study

How Two Ltd have collated some information in relation to some of the stationery purchases for the first six months of the year.

Month	Number of boxes of paper	Number of packs of document wallets
January	15	33
February	21	29
March	17	28
April	20	33
May	19	27
June	17	31

To work out the mode of the number of boxes of paper purchased in ascending order:

15, 17, 17, 19, 20, 21

The mode is 17 as this is the number that appears the most.

To work out the mode of the number of packs of document wallets purchased in descending order:

33, 33, 31, 29, 28, 27

The mode is 33 as this is the number that appears the most.

7.3 Calculating the mean

The mean is the most common measure of average. If you ask someone to find the average, this is the method they are most likely to use.

To calculate the mean (average) of a set of figures, you add up all of the numbers in the set of data given and then divide by how many numbers there are.

 Example

Bennett & Sons are looking at the profit that has been made by their branches in the UK for the first quarter of the year.

Branch	Profit
North Park	£15,987.56
South Park	£21,877.64
East Park	£12,563.22
West Park	£18,245.58

To work out the mean (average) profit:

Step One: Add up the total profit from each of the branches:

15,987.56 + 21,877.64 + 12,563.22 + 18,245.58 = 68,674.00

Step Two: Then divide the total by the number of branches:

68,674 ÷ 4 = 17,168.50

The mean (average) profit made by the branches is £17,168.50.

Note: You can check your answer by doing the following:

17,168.50 x 4 = 68,674

68,674 − 15,987.56 − 21,877.64 - 12,563.22 − 18,245.58 = 0

This means that your answer is correct.

But what happens if someone make a loss? This would mean that negative figures would come into the calculation. Adding a negative number is the same as subtracting the number (without the negative). For example 3 + (−2) = 3−2 = 1.

Example

Bennett & Sons are looking at the profit or loss made by North Park over the last year.

Rather than looking month on month, they have requested that the information be viewed in quarters.

North Park	Profit or Loss
January – March	-£3,485.75
April – June	£31,895.24
July – September	-£5,635.22
October - December	£54,251.79

To work out the mean (average) profit or loss per quarter:

Step One: Add up the total profit or loss over the year:

-£3,485.75 + £31,895.24 - £5,635.22 + £54,251.79 = 77,026.06

Step Two: Then divide the total by the number of quarters:

77,026.06 ÷ 4 = 19,256.515

The mean (average) profit made by North Park per quarter is £19,256.52 to 2 decimal places.

 Test your understanding 13

The Payroll Clerk has been asked to work out the averages of the hours worked by an employee in the production department in a week:

Day	Hours worked
Monday	8
Tuesday	7
Wednesday	8
Thursday	9
Friday	10

Calculate the following:

a)   The range of hours works

b)   The mode of hours worked

c)   The mean (average) number of hours worked (rounded to the nearest hour)

8 Identifying differences and checking results of calculations

8.1 Identifying differences between figures over time

 Case study

When looking at a set of figures Jessica may be asked to identify differences over a period of time. This would involve looking at the increases or decreases over the period.

 Example

Bennett & Sons are looking at the sales that have been made by South Park over the last year.

South Park	Profit
January	£15,872.51
February	£15,475.34
March	£17,233.32
April	£18,565.28
May	£15,227.84
June	£19,288.45
July	£18,799.73
August	£14,276.11
September	£16,993.21
October	£17,665.32
November	£18,325.45
December	£19,445.44

To work out the increase or decrease, you work out the difference between one month and the next. To do so, take the latest figure and subtract the previous figure from it e.g. February - January.

If the figure you are left with is a negative number it suggests a decrease, however if it is a positive number it suggests an increase.

South Park	Increase/Decrease	Amount
January - February	Decrease	£397.17
February – March	Increase	£1,757.98
March – April	Increase	£1,331.96
April – May	Decrease	£3,337.44
May – June	Increase	£4,060.61
June – July	Decrease	£488.72
July – August	Decrease	£4,523.62
August – September	Increase	£2,717.10
September – October	Increase	£672.11
October – November	Increase	£660.13
November - December	Increase	£1,119.99

8.2 Using estimation/rounding

Before working out a calculation, it is a good idea to estimate what you think that the answer will be. This will help to ensure that the answer you arrive at is accurate.

To do this you need to round the numbers. What you round the number to depends on the size of the figures you are working with; it could be to the nearest 10, 100 or 1,000.

Example

Bennett & Sons are looking at the wages for a member of the sales staff at West Park over a month. The person is paid £8.90 an hour.

	Hours worked	Rounded question	Estimated answer	Accurate answer
Week 1	42	40 x 9	£360	£373.80
Week 2	41	40 x 9	£360	£364.90
Week 3	34	30 x 9	£270	£302.60
Week 4	35	40 x 9	£360	£311.50
Total	152		£1,350	£1,352.80

The difference between the estimated answer and the accurate answer is **£2.80.**

Test your understanding 14

How Two Ltd are looking at the wages for the machine operatives in the factory of one of their depots over a week.

The machine operatives are paid £7.80 an hour.

	Hours worked	Rounded question	Estimated answer	Accurate answer
Monday	633			
Tuesday	742			
Wednesday	649			
Thursday	682			
Friday	724			
Total				

The difference between the estimated answer and the accurate answer is £..................

9 Summary and Interview Assessment

In this chapter we have looked at the common maths functions used in accounting and how numbers can be calculated and presented for business purposes.

You will need to practice the techniques learnt in the chapter to make sure you are able to perform the calculations quickly and confidently on a calculator. And, where needed, use the checking and estimating tools suggested to ensure your answer looks correct.

Returning to our case study, Jessica's interview assessment for the role at How Two Ltd now follows – see how well you can apply the numbers in business by completing it.

Case study activity 6 – Interview Assessment

Jessica has been set the following tasks to complete as part of her interview:

Task 1

Work out the mean, mode and range of the following estimated sales for the next 6 months:

January	February	March	April	May	June
10,000	9,500	14,000	13,500	14,000	15,500

Mean:

Mode:

Range:

Task 2

Below is a breakdown of the profit of one of our shops over the last 6 months:

January	February	March	April	May	June
4,500	5,000	6,750	6,900	6,300	5,400

Identify the increase/decrease in profit month on month:

Jan – Feb =

Feb – Mar =

Mar – Apr =

Apr – May =

May – Jun =

Task 3

Below are the hours worked for three members of staff at one of the shops. Calculate their total pay for the week.

Rate of pay £9.50 per hour					
	Mon	**Tue**	**Wed**	**Thu**	**Fri**
Jim	7 hours	5.5 hours	6 hours	7 hours	6 hours
Dave	8 hours	7.5 hours	4 hours	7.5 hours	5 hours
Ahmed	6 hours	7.5 hours	8 hours	8 hours	6.5 hours

Jim:

Dave:

Ahmed:

Task 4

Calculate the VAT and gross amounts of the following invoices and then write the gross figures as a fraction of the total for each invoice:

	Net	VAT	Total
Invoice 101	100.00		
Invoice 102	150.00		
Invoice 103	200.00		
Invoice 104	233.34		
Invoice 105	150.00		
Totals	833.34		

Fractions:

Invoice 101 =

Invoice 102 =

Invoice 103 =

Invoice 104 =

Invoice 105 =

Task 5

a)   Round the following quarterly sales and cost of sales figures to the nearest £'000.

b)   State the ratio of the sales figures to cost of sales

c)   Break the ratios down into their lowest form

	Jan - Mar	Apr - Jun	Jul - Sep	Oct - Dec
Sales	11,754	15,789	29,659	49,200
Cost of sales	3,256	7,770	6,250	6,825

Rounded

	Jan - Mar	Apr - Jun	Jul - Sep	Oct - Dec
Sales				
Cost of sales				

Ratios:

Jan – Mar =

Apr – Jun =

Jul – Sep =

Oct – Dec =

Answers to chapter activities

 Test your understanding 1

a) The weekly credit sales are £108,219.70

22300 + 23210.5 + 22225.2 + 24375 + 16010 =

108219.7

b) The weekly cash sales are £12,646.69

2499.99 + 3325.5 + 2769 + 2005 + 2047.2 =

12646.69

c) The total weekly sales are £120,866.39

108219.70 + 12646.69 =

120866.39

 Test your understanding 2

a) The total sales income is £284,942.10

258956.5 + 25985.6 =

284942.1

b) The gross profit is £129,726.75

284942.1 - 155215.35 =

129726.75

c) The net profit is £23,783.80

129726.75 - 65500 - 12576 - 10040.5 - 12875.7 - 4950.75 =

23783.8

Test your understanding 3

a)

	Hours worked	Pay per hour	Gross pay	*calculation*
Kamal	35	£7.20	£252.00	*35 x 7.2*
Pamela	35	£8.50	£297.50	*35 x 8.5*
Jason	16	£8.50	£136.00	*16 x 8.5*
Sana	8	£7.20	£57.60	*8 x 7.2*
	Total weekly gross pay		£743.10	*252. + 297.5 + 136.+ 57.6*

b) The total weekly gross pay is £743.10.

 Test your understanding 4

The total cost of Kamal's weekly wage was £216.00

Divided by the cost per hour £7.20

$216. \div 7.2 =$

30

Last week Kamal worked for **30 hours.**

 Test your understanding 5

$\underline{54,000} \times 3 = \textbf{32,400 black mouse mats.}$
  5

Test your understanding 6

How Two Ltd. has 45,000 customers

$\frac{2}{3}$ of customers pay on credit - 45,000 ÷ 3 x 2 = 30,000 credit customers.

The remainder must be cash customers – 45,000 – 30,000 = **15,000**

You can also work this out by calculating the fraction for cash customers. If credit customers account for $\frac{2}{3}$, cash customers must account for $\frac{1}{3}$ so 45,000 ÷ 3 x 1 = **15,000.**

 Test your understanding 7

Firstly, you need to determine how many people there are in total:

The Morris family has 5 members, the Kazee family has 4 members and the Thomas family has 2 members, so there are 11 people in total. This is the denominator.

The fraction of the total bill that the Morris family should pay is $\frac{5}{11}$, for the Kazee family it is $\frac{4}{11}$, and for the Thomas's it is $\frac{2}{11}$

The bill should be split as follows:

Morris family $\frac{210.56}{11}$ x 5 = 95.70909, a monetary value of £95.71

Kazee family $\frac{210.56}{11}$ x 4 = 76.56727, a monetary value of £76.57

Thomas family $\frac{210.56}{11}$ x 2 = 38.28363, a monetary value of £38.28

Check that the total bill will be paid correctly: 95.71 + 76.57 + 38.28 = 210.56

Test your understanding 8

Divide 125 by 25 to give an answer of 5.

We are comparing production *to* administration, so the ratio is written as **5:1.**

There are 5 times more employees who work in production than in administration.

 Test your understanding 9

Divide 225,000 by 75,000 = 3

We are comparing cost of sales *to* sales, so the ratio is expressed as **1:3**. For every £1 of cost of sales there are £3 of sales.

Test your understanding 10

Percentage	Fraction	Decimal
25%	$\frac{25}{100}$	**0.25**
2%	$\frac{2}{100}$	0.02
10%	$\frac{10}{100}$	0.10
1%	$\frac{1}{100}$	**0.01**
50%	$\frac{50}{100}$	0.50
5%	$\frac{5}{100}$	0.05

Test your understanding 11

How Two Ltd	
VAT NO. 456 7656 909	

Grange Theatre	Invoice no: 5678
Blackburn Avenue	Tax point: 23 September
Diggle	2017
LF2 689	

HDMI	£75.00
Less Discount 5%	**£3.75**
Total after discount	**£71.25**
VAT at 20%	**£14.25**
Total	**£85.50**

Payment terms: 7 days net

How Two Ltd	
VAT NO. 456 7656 909	

H Kazee	Invoice no: 35281
Bristol Street	Tax point: 26 September
Gloucester	2017
AL9 867	

5 HB78 @ £15.00	£75.00
10 AN5787 @ £2.30	£23.00
Sub total	**£98.00**
Less Discount 15%	**£14.70**
Total after discount	**£83.30**
VAT at 20%	**£16.66**
Total £99.96	

Payment terms: 7 days net

Note: VAT should always be rounded DOWN to the nearest penny.

Test your understanding 12

	No of employees	Percentage of the total number of employees	Calculation
Production department	8	**47.1%**	$\frac{8}{17}$ x 100 = 47.05 (rounded to 47.1)
Marketing department	3	**17.6%**	$\frac{3}{17}$ x 100 = 17.64 (rounded to 17.6)
Accounts department	2	**11.8%**	$\frac{2}{17}$ x 100 = 11.76 (rounded to 11.8)
Sales department	4	**23.5%**	$\frac{4}{17}$ x 100 = 23.52 (rounded to 23.5)
Total number of employees	17	**100%**	$\frac{17}{17}$ x 100 = 100

The total of all the individual percentages should always equal 100%.

Test your understanding 13

a) The range of hours worked = 10 – 7 = 3

b) The mode is 8

c) The mean number of hours worked is:

8 + 7 + 8 + 9 + 10 = 42

42 ÷ 5 = 8.4

The mean is 8 hours (rounded to the nearest hour)

Test your understanding 14

Day	Hours worked	Rounded question	Estimated answer	Accurate answer
Monday	633	630 x 8	£5,040	£4,937.40
Tuesday	742	740 x 8	£5,920	£5,787.60
Wednesday	649	650 x 8	£5,200	£5,062.20
Thursday	682	680 x 8	£5,440	£5,319.60
Friday	724	720 x 8	£5,760	£5,647.20
Total			£27,360	£26,754

The difference between the estimated answer and the accurate answer is **£606.**

 Case study activity 6 – Interview Assessment

Task 1

Mean: 10,000 + 9,500 + 14,000 + 13,500 + 14,000 + 15,500 = 76,500

76,500 / 6 = **12,750**

Mode: 14,000

Range: 15,500 – 9,500 = **6,000**

Task 2

Jan – Feb = Increased by £500

Feb – Mar = Increased by £1,750

Mar – Apr = Increased by £150

Apr – May = Decreased by £600

May – Jun = Decreased by £900

Task 3

Jim = 31.5 hours x 9.50 = £299.25

Dave = 32 hours x 9.50 = £304.00

Ahmed = 36 hours x 9.50 = £342.00

KAPLAN PUBLISHING

Task 4

	Net	VAT	Total
Invoice 101	100.00	20.00	120.00
Invoice 102	150.00	30.00	180.00
Invoice 103	200.00	40.00	240.00
Invoice 104	233.34	46.66	280.00
Invoice 105	150.00	30.00	180.00
Totals	833.34	166.66	1000.00

Fractions:

Invoice 101 = 120/1000 = 12/100 = 6/50 = 3/25

Invoice 102 = 180/1000 = 18/100 = 18/100 = 9/50

Invoice 103 = 240/1000 = 24/100 = 12/50 = 6/25

Invoice 104 = 280/1000 = 28/100 = 14/50 = 7/25

Invoice 105 = 180/1000 = 18/100 = 18/100 = 9/50

Task 5

Rounded

	Jan - Mar	Apr - Jun	Jul - Sep	Oct - Dec
Sales	12,000	16,000	30,000	49,000
Cost of sales	3,000	8,000	6,000	7,000

Jan – Mar = 12,000:3,000 = 12:3 = **4:1**

Apr – Jun = 16,000:8,000 = 16:8 = **2:1**

Jul – Sep = 30,000:6,000 = 30:6 = **5:1**

Oct – Dec = 49,000:7,000 = 49:7 = **7:1**

Developing skills for the workplace

4

Introduction

When you start a new job, you may be asked to complete an induction; this will introduce you to the company and their working practices. It will explain their key internal and external policies that must be adhered to by employees. It will also highlight the professional conduct that the organisation expects from its employees.

This chapter describes three of the most important aspects of professional behaviour: working with others, professional courtesy and how to keep sensitive information secure.

KNOWLEDGE	CONTENTS
Develop skills for the workplace	1 Professional behaviour
2.1 Working with others	2 Working with others
2.3 Professional behaviour	3 Confidentiality and data security
2.5 Understand the importance of keeping data and information secure	4 Summary and further questions

1 Professional behaviour

1.1 Case study: an introduction

 Case study

Jessica passed her maths assessment with flying colours and was successful at securing the job.

She was preparing to go and attend the organisation's induction day. She was looking forward to learning about the company rules/regulations and policies that she needed to adhere to.

1.2 Policies and procedures

Employees are expected to display certain personal attributes whilst at work. There will also be a number of policies and procedures that must be adhered to by all employees.

This helps to set a benchmark for professional behaviour in the workplace and ensures that all staff are behaving in a way that projects a positive image of themselves and the organisation.

These include:

Punctuality	Being punctual means being on time, both in terms of arriving at your place of work on time and completing a required task at an agreed time. Adhere to break times and do not leave work early.
Dress Code	If your employer has a dress code, ensure that you respect it and dress accordingly.
Reliability	Employers and your team workers will need to rely on you to do the work that you promised to do.
Willingness to learn	Showing a willingness to learn demonstrates to others that you are interested in your job role and the organisation. It also means that you are not afraid of learning new skills which will help you and the organisation to develop.

Social Media	Most companies state that computers in the workplace should not be used to access social media and that any online activity is for work related rather than personal use and therefore not for socialising. There is also a danger of a security breach or accidentally acquiring a computer virus that could disable the whole of the organisation's systems.
Personal Phones	As a general rule, it mobile phones are not allowed to be used during working hours. Therefore it is usually best to keep them on silent or switch them off.

Usually in the first couple of days of starting a job, you will attend what is called an induction.

 Definition

An induction is a short programme which introduces new employees to the working environment. This is where you are introduced to the organisation and you will learn about the company objectives and values. The process covers key regulations and policies which all employees must follow.

Typically, during an induction, new starters will then be taken through the policies and procedures relevant to their role, and usually receive a copy of an employee handbook. An employee handbook will contain lots of information about the company, but it will also detail all of the policies and procedures that must be adhered to as an employee of that company.

1.3 Health and safety in the workplace

New employees will receive health and safety training as part of their induction to the organisation. Everyone in the workplace has a duty of care to all employees, customers, visitors and anyone on the business premises. If an employer is found to be responsible for an injury, they may be held liable and legal action may be taken against the organisation.

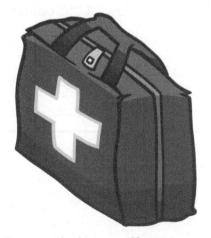

Because health and safety at work is so important all business organisations provide training and written rules that everyone should follow to reduce risks in the workplace. If you see something that is unsafe, or could cause an accident it is your responsibility to report it to your manager.

One way that you can help to maintain health and safety in the workplace is to keep your own work area clean and tidy. You should make sure that walkways are not blocked by boxes of papers, or trailing wires that could cause someone to trip. Many workers find themselves overwhelmed by the amount of clutter on their desks, so by taking a few minutes each day to tidy up your work area you can make your office surroundings more professional, healthier and less stressful.

Keeping your work area tidy will also help you to prevent any confidential information to be left lying around – the need to do this will be covered later in this chapter.

Test your understanding 1

Today is Marvin's first day in his new job. He has been told that he will have an induction day.

Which of the following should Marvin expect during the induction day (tick all that apply)?

	✓
A job interview	
Information about the company's policies	
An introduction to key staff in the company	
An overview of the company's values	
Lots of fun games and activities with other new starters	
To finish work early	
A promotion	

Test your understanding 2

Marvin's has been with his new employer for a week. He has been warned by a colleague about using his mobile phone during work hours. He is unsure of the company's policy regarding this.

Where should he look to find out? Tick the most appropriate answer.

	✓
The job specification	
The company handbook	
The company website	
A government employment website	

Test your understanding 3

Marvin overhears three statements from his colleagues in his first week with the company. For each one, decide if they are true or false and tick the correct box.

Statement	True	False
"As we work at a desk in the office and not in the warehouse, health and safety is not relevant to us."		
"Don't worry about that loose cable next to your desk – it is not your responsibility to report it."		
"Everyone here has a duty of care to keep things safe for both our colleagues and visitors".		

Test your understanding 4

Health and safety in the workplace is the responsibility of:

	✓
The government	
The managers	
The employees	
The managers and the employees	

1.4   Polite communication with colleagues and customers

It is important to portray yourself in a polite and professional manner at all times in the workplace. Communication in the most important attribute in business as it helps the effective and efficient operation of a successful organisation.

For example, when in meetings it is important to engage fully with what is being communicated. If you don't listen properly, you could miss a vital piece of information that is relevant to you successfully completing a task. It projects an image to the employer of someone who is disinterested in their role and who doesn't take it seriously.

An excellent communicator will become an integral part of the team who others can rely on. This is important if you want to progress within your career.

The following principles of polite communication should be followed:

Use correct names	In the workplace it may be acceptable to address your colleagues by their first name unless they direct otherwise. When speaking to customers remain respectful, address them as Sir/ Madam/ Mr/ Mrs/ Miss.
Listen to the other person	Show an interest in what the other person is saying. Maintain eye contact when speaking face to face. Never interrupt someone when they are on the telephone or face to face.
Appropriate language	Avoid the use of slang terms, swearing and offensive humour
Remember your manners	It is important to be courteous both in terms of words and actions. For example, use 'please' and 'thank you' wherever necessary/appropriate and hold the door open for those behind you. Likewise, shaking hands when you first meet a customer is considered sound business etiquette.

Test your understanding 5

A key client, Tony Foster, the Managing Director of Bolsover Breweries has called to raise a complaint with an invoice. Having spoken to one of Marvin's colleagues, the call has been put through to Marvin for him to advise the customer.

Which is the best way for Marvin to start the conversation? Tick the most suitable answer.

	✓
Good morning Mr Foster. This is Marvin. How can I help?	
Good morning Tony. How's things there?	
This is Marvin speaking. How can I help?	
Hi Sir. How's things there?	
Hello Mr Bolsover. How can I help?	

 Test your understanding 6

Which of the following suggest that Marvin is listening to others when they are in a department meeting? Tick the TWO most appropriate answers.

	✓
He is constantly checking his watch to ensure that he can get back to focus on his e-mails	
He asks further questions based on the comments made by this manager	
He becomes easily distracted by a chart of sales figures on the wall of the room	
He often completes one of his colleague's sentences to save time, assuming he knows what he is going to say	
He makes notes as other people speak and occasionally nods when a key point is made	

Test your understanding 7

Which of the following would NOT be appropriate if you were meeting an important customer for the first time (tick ALL that apply)?

	✓
Shaking hands with the customer and introducing yourself to him	
Calling the customer by his first name despite having not met him previously	
Crossing your arms and shaking your head when you do not agree with what the customer is saying	
Smiling and making eye contact as the customer tells you about their company's history	
Showing the customer something that made you laugh on social media, which is not work-related	
Swearing about one of the customer's competitors who do not use your company as a supplier	
Appearing comfortable by slouching in the chair, with your legs crossed in a relaxed manner	

KAPLAN PUBLISHING

2 Working with others

2.1 Team working skills

Each department within an organisation is subdivided into teams so that all the work can be shared out to ensure it is completed on time. Team working means that the work will be completed more efficiently and effectively rather than each individual working independently.

🔍 Definition

A team is more than a group of individuals. A team can be described as any group of people who must significantly relate with each other in order to accomplish shared, specified aims.

Therefore a team usually:

* shares a common goal
* is committed to achieving that goal
* enjoys working together to achieve it.

To be able to work effectively in a team you will need to develop good team working skills. These skills include mutual support for each other; respect for others opinions, and the sharing of information. Where working effectively, the members of a team show collective loyalty and possess a strong sense of **team spirit.**

The team leader will allocate the tasks that the team needs to complete to individual members of the team. Each member of the team will then have certain tasks to do by a specific deadline. It is therefore important to identify what your specific role and responsibility is within the team. In some instances, other members of your team will need information from you before they can complete their work; this puts you in a position of trust. To ensure that the organisation as a whole can operate successfully, co-operation amongst you and your colleagues is key.

There are usually realistic deadlines to work towards. It is therefore important that you share good communication skills with the team, so that everybody is aware if a task may not be completed on time.

If something happens which means that the team cannot complete a task on time, the team leader will have a **contingency plan.** For example, the team leader may build in some spare time in each team member's weekly schedule to allow them to step in to help other individuals if something has happened which means that they cannot keep to the planned schedule

Effective leadership and staff co-operating collaboratively in this way promotes a positive working environment. This can assist in keeping team morale high, which in turn can increase productivity as the team work towards common goals and success for the organisation.

 Definitions

Leadership is an influence directed toward the achievement of a goal or goals. Leadership is therefore is concerned with setting goals and then inspiring people to achieve them.

 Test your understanding 8

Which of the following are characteristics of an effective team?

a)   Mutual respect and support

b)   Lack of communication

c)   Clear aims and allocated tasks

d)   Dominant individual members

e)   No obvious team leader

 Test your understanding 9

Which FOUR of the following are benefits of good team working?

	✓
Increased motivation of staff	
Higher staff morale	
Better staff pay	
More team leaders	
Better use of a mixture of skills	
Tighter control over staff	
More staff doing other people's work for them	
Increased productivity and success for the organisation	

3 Confidentiality and data security

3.1 Confidentiality

Most of the information supplied by the accounting function will be financial information that may be both sensitive and/or private. Whether the information is held on paper or held electronically on a computer, accounting staff must make sure that confidential information is kept in a safe and secure way, so that it is only made available to the people authorised to see it.

3.2 Commercial information

Information held by the accounts department may be commercially sensitive. For example, the price paid for a particular product, or discounts given to customers. If a competitor of the business knew this information they might be able to use it as a competitive advantage. It is therefore imperative to protect customer information.

3.3 Personal information

Personal information held about individuals, such as employees and customers, is protected by law. The Data Protection Act sets out rules about how personal data can be used.

The Act sets out eight data protection principles which must be followed when processing personal data.

The information must be:

1. used fairly and lawfully

2. used for limited, specifically stated purposes

3. used in a way that is adequate, relevant and not excessive

4. accurate

5. kept for no longer than is absolutely necessary

6. handled according to people's data protection rights

7. kept safe and secure

8. not transferred outside the European Economic Area without adequate protection

Any organisations who process personal data must register with the Information Commissioner's Office in order to be permitted to process data. The Information Commissioner's Office (ICO) is the UK's independent body set up to uphold information rights. You can find out how personal information is protected by visiting their website: https://www.ico.org.uk

Whether personal and sensitive information is held on computer or in a paper based filing system it must be kept safe and secure. This means it must be kept away from any unauthorised access. It would be wrong to leave personal data open to be viewed by just anyone.

Test your understanding 10

Tick the appropriate box for the statements provided:

Commercial information is information that can be sold to anyone, so it does not have to be kept confidential.

True ☐ or False ☐

You have finished working on a document, you have made notes on paper that you do not need anymore. Are you going to:

Discard the paper in the bin ☐   Shred the paper ☐

3.4 The security of confidential information

Advances in technology have enabled organisations to process more and more personal data, and to share information more easily. This has obvious benefits, but it also gives rise to equally obvious security risks.

If data is not properly safeguarded, this can seriously damage an organisation's reputation and compromise the safety of individuals.

If you have been given sensitive information to work with it is your responsibility to keep it safe and secure. Below are some examples of how you can keep confidential information secure in the situations you will find in an accounting office.

Example

Situation	Paper based filing system	Information held on a computer
Confidential information you are currently working with.	Any confidential information you are responsible for should be kept close by you at all times so that you are aware if anyone tries to read it. To avoid the information being seen by anyone passing by your desk, all confidential paperwork should be kept face down or in a folder until you need to work with it.	You may need to change the position of your computer screen to make sure that unauthorised people cannot see information on your computer screen as you are working. If this is not possible, you may need to move desks or offices to ensure that you can carry out the work. Sensitive information held on computers should be protected by multi-level passwords so that employees only see what is relevant to them. Never share your password with unauthorised people.
If you have to leave your workstation	If you have to leave your desk always put any confidential papers in a locked drawer or filing cabinet.	You should use the screen lock on your computer so that confidential information cannot be read by people passing your desk when you are away.
Storage of confidential information	Sensitive information should be kept in a locked filing cabinet, until it is needed.	Regular back-ups of computer data should be taken and stored in fireproof cabinets.
Out of date information	When confidential information is no longer needed it should be shredded before being recycled.	Data should be removed or deleted from computers by authorised staff from the Information Technology (IT) department.

Definition

Authorised person – Someone who has been given permission to do something on somebody else's behalf. For example, an employee who has been authorised to input confidential information onto a computer.

3.5 Passwords

Within an organisation you will have many passwords for different systems and processes. For example, you will have a password to be able to gain access to the computer system itself, you will then need another password to gain access to the accounting software and the chances are that other documents will be password protected for you to be able to view them.

It is important that you keep your password safe and secure and change it regularly in line with the company procedures or immediately if you suspect that someone has found out what your password is. You should avoid the use of names or dates that are personal to you as quite often these can be easy to guess. Ideally you should create a password that contains both upper and lower case letters, numbers and symbols. The harder it is for someone to guess your password, the harder it is for them to access sensitive information.

 Test your understanding 11

You have recently set up online banking for your current account.

You need to set a password for access to the online banking facilities. Which of the following would make a good password? Tick the TWO best answers from the options given.

	✓
Something you cannot remember	
Something other people are not likely to know	
Something obvious	
The word 'password'	
Your name and year of birth	
A combination of letters, numbers and symbols	
Something you saved on your PC in a file called Passwords	

Test your understanding 12

Below is a list of statements. State which are true and which are false.

Statement	True/False
Passwords can be shared with colleagues who are doing the same type work.	
All cabinet drawers with personal or commercial information in should be kept locked.	
If leaving your work station, you must ensure that the screen is blank and computer access blocked.	

3.6 Backups

It is important that regular backups are taking of the data within an organisation. Usually a company will take a backup of the information held on their server at least once a day. There should be more than one copy of the back up in case one of them becomes corrupt. A copy of the backup data should be kept in a fireproof cabinet or taken of site in case of an unexpected disaster such as a fire or a flood.

3.7 Anti-virus software

Anti-virus software is another key way in which an organisation can keep confidential information safe and secure. This is a piece of software that is installed into the computer system which will then scan information such as emails for viruses and will block any content that appears suspect. Viruses can be extremely dangerous as they can shut down a whole system in a very short space of time. If data becomes corrupt, you will not be able to see or use it therefore it is very important that an organisation protects itself with anti-virus software.

Test your understanding 13

You have been working on a confidential document on your computer and have to leave the office for ten minutes to deal with a customer. How can you keep the information on your screen confidential?

	✓
Switch the computer off	
Use the screen lock facility to lock the computer screen	
Stay at your desk	
Put some papers over the screen to hide the information	

> ### Test your understanding 14
>
> **Complete the following sentences:**
>
> a) I need to go to the bathroom, I should use my computer _____ lock.
>
> b) I have finished with this confidential paper so I am going to _____ it.
>
> c) I don't want anyone to read this paperwork so I am going to put it _____ on my desk.
>
> d) _____ software is another way of keeping information safe and secure.
>
> e) Backed up computer data should be stored in _____ cabinets.

3.8 Ethical behaviour

Behaving ethically means doing the right thing at the right time. As we have seen in this chapter, accounting professionals are trusted by their employers to handle confidential and sensitive information in an appropriate manner.

Confidentiality is one of the key ethical principles set out in the AAT's ethical guidelines (see http://www.aatethics.org.uk/code/).

The other fundamental ethical principles which form part of these guidelines are:

- **Objectivity** – accountants should remain independent and show sound judgement rather than allowing bias, personal interests or pressure from others to influence them.

- **Integrity** - this means being straightforward and honest when you perform your duties.

- **Professional behaviour and competence** – this means that you are able to perform your job to an acceptable level and provide a good service. All accounting professionals should undergo regular training to keep their technical knowledge up-to-date so that they can complete work to agreed standards, without mistakes.

4 Summary and further questions

This chapter has explained how to conduct yourself in a polite and professional manner in the workplace. You should be aware of policies and procedures relevant within your role and have a good understanding of confidentiality and keeping data safe.

We have also explained the importance of team working and communication within a team and you should understand that having respect for colleagues and peers is important.

Let us know return to Jessica's experience as she starts her employment with How Two Ltd.

 Case study activity 7

As part of her induction, Jessica has been provided with the staff handbook to detail the How Two Ltd's company policies. In the first week of her job, she sees her colleagues both keeping to the rules and breaking them.

For each of the statements below, indicate which policy is being addressed by entering the correct letter in the box from the pick list below. Also put a tick for good practice and a cross where the policy is not being kept to.

Statement	Policy	✓ / X
I knew you would be here! I knew you wouldn't let me down		
No, you cannot see if anyone has shared or commented on your post in work time		
I am so glad you're always on time or early, we will get to see the start		
No, I can't come to work in my jeans and t-shirt, the boss wouldn't like it		
Gosh you're keen, I've only just given you that work and you've done it already		
You had better switch that off, I can hear it vibrating in your pocket even though it's on silent		

Pick list

a) Punctuality   b) Dress Code   c) Reliability

d) Willingness to learn   e) Social Media   f) Personal Phones

---

Case study activity 8

Jessica has been asked to create her own unique password for the accounting system.

Which of the following passwords should she use?

a)   Password123

b)   JHoward011200

c)   JessHowTw0

d)   4yXkj2fR!*

 Case study activity 9

During a conversation in the staff canteen, several members of staff were discussing their rates of pay and the company bonus.

One of them, Neelam is upset that other people are being paid more than her. She asks Jessica to find out for her if one of her colleagues, Jason, is indeed being paid more than her.

What reply should Jessica give?

Statement	Correct?
Jessica confirms the amount that Jason does indeed receive more money than Neelam.	
Jessica tells Neelam that she will speak to her manager to see if she can tell her the information.	
Jessica explains to Neelam that this information is confidential and cannot be disclosed.	
Jessica ensures that all pay rates are accessible to all employees to avoid any future debate.	

Answers to chapter activities

📝 Test your understanding 1

	✓
A job interview	
Information about the company's policies	✓
An introduction to key staff in the company	✓
An overview of the company's values	✓
Lots of fun games and activities with other new starters	
To finish work early	
A promotion	

📝 Test your understanding 2

	✓
The job specification	
The company handbook	✓
The company website	
A government employment website	

📝 Test your understanding 3

Statement	True	False
"As we work at a desk in the office and not in the warehouse, health and safety is not relevant to us."		✓
"Don't worry about that loose cable next to your desk – it is not your responsibility to report it."		✓
"Everyone here has a duty of care to keep things safe for both our colleagues and visitors".	✓	

Test your understanding 4

	✓
The government	
The managers	
The employees	
The managers and the employees	✓

Test your understanding 5

	✓
Good morning Mr Foster. This is Marvin. How can I help?	✓
Good morning Tony. How's things there?	
This is Marvin speaking. How can I help?	
Hi Sir. How's things there?	
Hello Mr Bolsover. How can I help?	

Test your understanding 6

	✓
He is constantly checking his watch to ensure that he can get back to focus on his e-mails	
He asks further questions based on the comments made by this manager	✓
He becomes easily distracted by a chart of sales figures on the wall of the room	
He often completes one of his colleague's sentences to save time, assuming he knows what he is going to say	
He makes notes as other people speak and occasionally nods when a key point is made	✓

Test your understanding 7

	✓
Shaking hands with the customer and introducing yourself to him	
Calling the customer by his first name despite having not met him previously	✓
Crossing your arms and shaking your head when you do not agree with what the customer is saying	✓
Smiling and making eye contact as the customer tells you about their company's history	
Showing the customer something that made you laugh on social media, which is not work-related	✓
Swearing about one of the customer's competitors who do not use your company as a supplier	✓
Appearing comfortable by slouching in the chair, with your legs crossed in a relaxed manner	✓

Test your understanding 8

The following are characteristics of an effective team:

Mutual respect and support (a)

Clear aims and allocated tasks (c)

Test your understanding 9

	✓
Increased motivation of staff	✓
Higher staff morale	✓
Better staff pay	
More team leaders	
Better use of a mixture of skills	✓
Tighter control over staff	
More staff doing other people's work for them	
Increased productivity and success for the organisation	✓

Test your understanding 10

Commercial information is information that can be sold to anyone, so it does not have to be kept confidential.

True ☐ or False ☑

You have finished working on a document, you have made notes on paper that you do not need anymore. Are you going to:

Discard the paper in the bin ☐   Shred the paper ☑

Test your understanding 11

	✓
Something you cannot remember	
Something other people are not likely to know	✓
Something obvious	
The word 'password'	
Your name and year of birth	
A combination of letters, numbers and symbols	✓
Something you saved on your PC in a file called Passwords	

Test your understanding 12

Statement	True/False
Passwords can be shared with colleagues who are doing the same type work.	False
All cabinet drawers with personal or commercial information in should be kept locked.	True
If leaving your work station, you must ensure that the screen is blank and computer access blocked.	True

📝 Test your understanding 13

	✓
Switch the computer off	
Use the screen lock facility to lock the computer screen	✓
Stay at your desk	
Put some papers over the screen to hide the information	

📝 Test your understanding 14

a) I need to go to the bathroom, I should use my computer **screen lock**.

b) I have finished with this confidential paper so I am going to **shred** it.

c) I don't want anyone to read this paperwork so I am going to put it **face down** on my desk.

d) **Anti-virus** software is another way of keeping information safe and secure.

e) Backed up computer data should be stored in **fireproof** cabinets.

📖 Case study activity 7

Statement	Policy	✓ / X
I knew you would be here! I knew you wouldn't let me down	c	✓
No, you cannot see if anyone has shared or commented on your post in work time	e	X
I am so glad you're always on time or early, we will get to see the start	a	✓
No, I can't come to work in my jeans and t-shirt, the boss wouldn't like it	b	✓
Gosh you're keen, I've only just given you that work and you've done it already	d	✓
You had better switch that off, I can hear it vibrating in your pocket even though it's on silent	f	X

Case study activity 8

She should use:

d)   4yXkj2fR!*

 Case study activity 9

Statement	Correct?
Jessica confirms the amount that Jason does indeed receive more money than Neelam.	
Jessica tells Neelam that she will speak to her manager to see if she can tell her the information.	
Jessica explains to Neelam that this information is confidential and cannot be disclosed.	✓
Jessica ensures that all pay rates are accessible to all employees to avoid any future debate.	

Time management and communication skills

5

Introduction

Time management and communication skills are key traits to being successful in the workplace. This chapter will focus on these two key sets of skills, without which individuals cannot work effectively or efficiently.

In this chapter you will learn about the different tools and techniques to help you prioritise your workload. You will also learn about the different methods of communication within an office environment and how these should be presented in business.

KNOWLEDGE
Develop skills for the workplace
2.2 Time management
2.4 Workplace communication

CONTENTS
1   Time management
2   Planning aids
3   Communication skills
4   Written communication methods
5   Verbal communication methods
6   Spreadsheets and software for workplace communications
7   Summary and further questions

1 Time management

1.1 Case study: an introduction

 Case study

Jessica now feels that she has a good understanding of How Two Ltd as an organisation and the policies and procedures relevant to her.

She is now learning about some of the administrative tasks involved within her role and how to communicate information in different forms.

She is also aware of the importance of deadlines within a finance department and is keen to ensure that she applies the correct time management techniques to ensure that she completes her work on time.

1.2 The importance of time management

🔍 **Definition**

Time management is the process of planning and controlling the amount of time that is spent on specific activities, usually with the aim of increasing your efficiency or productivity.

As we saw in the previous chapter, each employee within a team will be allocated tasks to complete.

It is then up to those individuals to organise their own workload so that they can make sure that these tasks are completed efficiently within the deadlines set by the team leader. In order to do this, they will need to use their time management skills.

1.3 Deadlines

It is important that you manage your time effectively as failure to meet a deadline can have a detrimental effect on the rest of the team. If you do not complete your allocated work on time, the next person in line will be delayed and the overall deadline for completion will not be met.

If you feel that you are going to struggle to meet a deadline it is really important to raise it with your manager as soon as possible. This will enable a plan to put in place for other members of the team to help with the task to ensure that the deadline can still be met.

Some deadlines may be classed as urgent, the work will be allocated appropriately and you will be informed of what should be classed as an 'urgent' task. You should plan allocated work based on the time available and prioritise your tasks in accordance with its urgency or importance. For example, if your manager has asked you to assist with month-end procedures and it is the end of the month, you will need to prioritise this as an important task and therefore complete it as soon as possible. This is because the month-end figures will be needed to generate the Management Accounts which will need to be presented to the Directors by a specific date.

2 Planning aids

2.1 Methods of planning

A work plan is simply a list of jobs to complete, organised into the order in which they will be tackled and the time when each will be completed. There are many different methods which can be used to plan your work and the ones you choose may depend on your own personal preference, or be recommended by your team leader.

Some common planning methods which can be used on their own or in combination are:

Some common planning methods which can be used in combination are:

To do Lists / Check Lists

A 'to do' list is a simple check list of all the activities that need to be carried out each day. The first five minutes of each day are set aside to write out the 'to do' list, and as each activity is completed it is crossed off the list. If anything is not completed that day, it can be added to the 'to do' list for the next day. However, if there is a task which cannot be completed within a certain time, then you will need to let your team leader know so that they can reschedule the task if necessary.

💡 **Example**

> ## THINGS TO DO TODAY
>
> Date.......................
>
> 1 .... ☐
> 2 .... ☐
> 3 .... ☐
> 4 .... ☐
> 5 .... ☐
> 6 .... ☐
> 7 .... ☐

In Tray

You may have a set of letter trays on your workstation which can be used to organise the different types of documents you are working on.

For example, your job role may involve dealing with purchase orders, purchase delivery notes and purchase invoices. Each tray should be labelled accordingly for each different document so that you, and other members of the team, can find the documents quickly and easily.

A traditional method of using letter trays is to have three trays labelled 'In', 'Out' and 'Pending'. Any new documentation that you receive is put in the 'In' tray, any work that you cannot complete because you need information from someone else is placed in the 'Pending' tray, and any work that has completed and needs filing or passing on to another team member is placed in the 'Out' tray.

Each tray should be clearly labelled so that anyone leaving a document for you can put it into the correct tray without disturbing your work.

Diary

Team members may use individual diaries or a team diary to make a note of tasks that need to be completed on a certain date. For example, you may have a conversation with a customer who has been late in paying an invoice. You can make a note in the diary for a particular

time on a day next week to check if the customer's payment has been received.

Weekly Work Schedule

A schedule is a breakdown of the routine activities you need to complete for the following week as agreed with your team leader. The schedule should include all the planned activities for the week.

Example

	Monday	Tuesday	Wednesday	Thursday	Friday
9am - 10am	Opening and distributing post	Opening and distributing post	Opening and distributing post	Opening and distributing post	Opening and distributing post
10am – 11am	Processing Purchase Orders	Processing Sales Invoices	Processing Purchase Orders	Processing Sales Invoices	Team meeting
11am – 12pm	Processing Purchase Orders	Processing Sales Invoices	Processing Purchase Orders	Processing Sales Invoices	Preparing customers statement of accounts
12pm – 1pm	Preparing Banking	Preparing Banking	Preparing Banking	Preparing Banking	Preparing Banking
1pm – 2pm	Lunch	Lunch	Lunch	Lunch	Lunch
2pm – 3pm	Dealing with email queries	Dealing with email queries	Dealing with email queries	Dealing with email queries	Dealing with email queries
3pm – 4pm	Departmental Reports	Preparing supplier payments	Departmental Reports	Preparing supplier payments	Reconcile Petty Cash
4pm – 5pm	Filing documents	Filing documents	Filing documents	Filing documents	Filing documents

It is important that everyone keeps their colleagues and line managers informed of their progress against deadlines. If a deadline is not met, or is in danger of not being met, this will need to be communicated at the earliest opportunity and in an appropriate manner.

Calendars

Calendars come in various formats; there are many free printable types on the internet. Below is an example of a weekly calendar - ensure that you choose one with plenty of space for writing your information if this is the sort of calendar you choose. Calendars also could be monthly or yearly, but these are less useful for planning daily or routine tasks due to a lack of space and specific timeframes for each day.

Example

A weekly calendar:

Monday **26**	Tuesday **27**	Wednesday **28**	Thursday **29**	Friday **30**	Saturday **31**	Sunday **1**
6:00 Boxing Day	6:00 Substitute day	6:00	6:00	6:00	6:00	6:00 New Year's Day
7:00	7:00	7:00	7:00	7:00	7:00	7:00
8:00	8:00	8:00	8:00	8:00	8:00	8:00
9:00	9:00	9:00	9:00	9:00	9:00	9:00
10:00	10:00	10:00	10:00	10:00	10:00	10:00
11:00	11:00	11:00	11:00	11:00	11:00	11:00
12:00	12:00	12:00	12:00	12:00	12:00	12:00
1:00	1:00	1:00	1:00	1:00	1:00	1:00
2:00	2:00	2:00	2:00	2:00	2:00	2:00
3:00	3:00	3:00	3:00	3:00	3:00	3:00
4:00	4:00	4:00	4:00	4:00	4:00	4:00
5:00	5:00	5:00	5:00	5:00	5:00	5:00
6:00	6:00	6:00	6:00	6:00	6:00	6:00
7:00	7:00	7:00	7:00	7:00	7:00	7:00
8:00	8:00	8:00	8:00	8:00	8:00	8:00
9:00	9:00	9:00	9:00	9:00	9:00	9:00
10:00	10:00	10:00	10:00	10:00	10:00	10:00
11:00	11:00	11:00	11:00	11:00	11:00	11:00

As the example shows, a calendar is a good way of breaking up your day in terms of time.

Nowadays, many people have a smart phone with an integrated calendar or one as part of their email package at work.

Scheduling tasks in a calendar such as this allows a function whereby reminders can be set at a time prior to a task starting. For example, if you have a meeting scheduled for 10:00am, you can set yourself a reminder for 30 minutes prior to the meeting. Your reminder would then pop up on your computer screen or phone which will then give you time to prepare anything you need to take with you or will give you time to arrive at your meeting on time.

Test your understanding 1

Jodie is a member of the Purchase Ledger team at How Two Ltd. Jessica is shadowing her for the morning to learn about the administrative side of the job and pick up tips on time management.

Jodie has a series of necessary administrative tasks to complete in the morning before a large departmental meeting in the afternoon. Her manager Julie has informed her that the meeting is extremely important.

Tick the ONE most appropriate solution for Jodie from the list provided.

	✓
Jodie should do the straightforward jobs and leave the more difficult ones for her colleagues to complete after she has left for the meeting.	
Jodie should make a list of all that she needs to do in the morning and give each a timescale and priority.	
Jodie should realise that it will be difficult to perform all of the tasks so she should put them all off until the next day.	
Jodie should ignore the regional meeting and devote all her time to the tasks she needs to complete in the office.	

 Test your understanding 2

Thomas has three tasks to complete, each of which will take two hours. His supervisor is expecting him to have completed them all by 10am tomorrow. Thomas was unable to perform any of the tasks this morning because his computer was not working. It is now 2pm. Thomas goes home at 5pm.

What should Thomas do in these circumstances?

A   Complete one of the tasks and start one of the others. He should be able to complete all of them by noon tomorrow.

B   Complete the most urgent task and take home the other two tasks. He is bound to be able to find time to finish them tonight.

C   Contact his supervisor immediately and explain the problem. He should suggest that he finishes what he considers to be the most urgent task first before starting one of the others.

D   Start all of the tasks and do parts of each of them. This way he has at least done something towards each of them before he goes home.

Test your understanding 3

Jodie has given Jessica a list of her tasks for the following week and has asked Jessica to have a go at putting these into a work schedule for her. She informed Jessica that she usually takes her lunch from 1pm until 2pm.

Jodie has told her not to worry - it is simply a training exercise - so she just wants to see how well Jessica is picking up the time management techniques.

Task list:

Check emails (must be done first thing every morning) – 1 hour

Checking supplier invoices – 2 hours each day

Supplier payment run – 2 hours on a Friday

Processing purchase orders – 2 hours each day except Fridays

Purchase Ledger Meeting – 2 hours at 10am Friday

Supplier account reconciliations – 3 hours anytime

Purchase Ledger reports – 1 hour

Filing documents – 4 hours

Enter the above tasks into the work schedule below, ensuring that all deadlines are met

	Monday	Tuesday	Wednesday	Thursday	Friday
9am - 10am					
10am – 11am					
11am – 12pm					
12pm – 1pm					
1pm – 2pm	Lunch	Lunch	Lunch	Lunch	Lunch
2pm – 3pm					
3pm – 4pm					
4pm – 5pm					

3 Communication skills

3.1 Case study: an introduction

 Case study

Having shadowed other members of staff at How Two Ltd, Jessica becomes aware of the importance of communication between both herself and her colleagues (internal) and between How Two Ltd employees and their suppliers and customers.

Jessica starts to consider the different types of communication and the software she can use in order to deliver business communications. She realises that different methods of communication will be better served to different types of task.

3.2 Formal and informal communication

 Definition

Communication is the two-way interchange of information, ideas, facts and emotions by one or more persons.

Typically business communication is either written or verbal (spoken), however communication can take place without any words at all, through body language (non-verbal communication).

There are various methods of communication. Accounting professionals will need to communicate regularly with internal and external customers and it is essential that you use an appropriate acceptable method for both of these groups. Poor communication can create an adverse impression of the organisation.

There are many different types of business documents that you will come upon in an accounting environment. The following should help you to identify the correct style to use:

Formal Language

Business English is the formal language used for business communications, especially when producing documents. Formal language is structured and professional and follows accepted grammatical rules and spelling conventions. You should not use slang or text language and words are written out in full and not abbreviated.

Informal Language

Informal language is a more casual means of communication and is less structured than formal language. It is most often used in speech, whether face-to-face or on the telephone. In some cases, it may be acceptable to use informal language in a business setting, for example when you are communicating with your peers. However, even when communicating with people you know well it is still possible for your message to be misunderstood if you use slang or text language. If you are in any doubt you should always use formal language.

Formal language is most commonly used with external customers. Informal language may be used when communicating with internal customers. However, even when using informal language you should make sure that the message is clear and easily understandable.

Test your understanding 4

Decide when you would use these examples of formal or informal language.

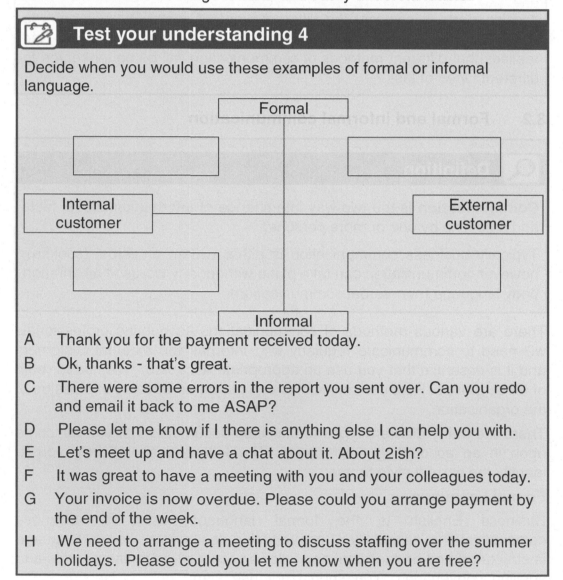

A   Thank you for the payment received today.

B   Ok, thanks - that's great.

C   There were some errors in the report you sent over. Can you redo and email it back to me ASAP?

D   Please let me know if I there is anything else I can help you with.

E   Let's meet up and have a chat about it. About 2ish?

F   It was great to have a meeting with you and your colleagues today.

G   Your invoice is now overdue. Please could you arrange payment by the end of the week.

H   We need to arrange a meeting to discuss staffing over the summer holidays. Please could you let me know when you are free?

Test your understanding 5

Classify the following communication activities as:

- formal or informal
- internal or external

	Formal / Informal	Internal / External
A letter to a member of the public responding to a complaint		
Asking a colleague whether or not an order has been fulfilled		
A report for the directors analysing annual business performance		
A Human Resources policy document for all staff		
An e-mail to all customers regarding a new invoicing system		

---

4 Written communication methods

4.1 The use of e-mails in business

E-mails are an effective way to communicate formal or informal information electronically to internal and external customers. Many business people receive hundreds of e-mails every day and find dealing with emails very  time consuming. It is important that any business emails you send are short and to the point so that they can be read and responded to quickly.

4.2 Effective e-mail format

E-mails should have a clear subject line and the message itself should be clear and concise. Some people recommend writing the message in no more than five sentences so that the recipient is more likely to read the e-mail and respond quickly. If an e-mail contains detailed information, it may be more suitable to include the additional information as an attachment.

🔍 **Definition**

Attachment – An email attachment is a computer file, for example a document or spreadsheet, which is sent with an e-mail message.

Although e-mails are less formal that a printed business letter you should always write emails with the same care that you would use to write a formal letter. Remember that people are unlikely to be offended if you are too formal, but some may think you are being rude if you are too informal.

To: renbow@abc.net

Cc: accountsteam@newoft.co.uk

Subject: Returned faulty goods

Hello Jack

Further to our conversation today, I can confirm that the goods you returned to us have been received in our warehouse.

The warehouse team will check that the goods are faulty and, if so, we will send a credit note to you immediately.

Kind regards,

A. Wyatt

Accounts Administrator

📝 **Test your understanding 6**

Which of the following should always be present in business e-mail correspondence (tick all which apply):

	✓
A clear and purposeful subject heading	
Slang words	
Simple and well-structured content	
Jokes and personal comments	
Capital letters to stress the importance of your thoughts	
An appropriate sign off	

4.3 Business writing

Business documents follow a standard structure according to organisational guidelines.

In each case, they should be in the correct format, using clear and concise language, and they should be free from any grammatical or spelling mistakes.

4.4 Paragraphs and structure in business documents

All business documents should be structured by using paragraphs. Paragraphs help the reader to understand your message because:

- They break text down into manageable proportions

- Each sentence in a paragraph relates to the same topic

- Starting a new paragraph makes it clear to the reader that you are moving on to another topic.

In business documents there should be a short introductory paragraph; followed by one or two paragraphs with the main content. The final paragraph should be a short conclusion.

When writing business communications the pneumonic STRIPE is a useful structure to follow:

S	Salutation	A greeting, for example 'Dear ....'
T	Topic	The heading or subject
R	Reason	The main purpose of the communication
I	Information	Specific details or a request for information
P	Prompt to action	What you would like the reader to do.
E	End	A complimentary close and signature

4.5 The use of letters in business

Letters are used to communicate with **external** customers and should always be written using **formal** language.

All letters contain similar elements. However, you should also check your organisation's guidelines as it is important that all letters sent out by employees of the organisation are consistent with the organisation's house style.

Definition

House Style - A set of guidelines that explain how all documents produced by an organisation should be set out.

Letterheads and return addresses

Many organisations have a letterhead which contains the company logo, the postal address, and company website address.

If your organisation does not have a letterhead, the name and address of the organisation should appear on the right side of the document, immediately above the date line in the letter.

House styles and templates

Before producing any business documents you should check whether your organisation has a house style and if it has you should always follow those guidelines.

House style guidelines could include:

Font	The type, size and colour of font to be used for normal text. The house style may also define the size and formatting of any headings and the type of bullet points to use.
Addresses	A house style may state where addresses should appear on a letter and whether they should include punctuation.
Days and dates	The correct order and style for the date may be given. For example, one house style may state that just the number is given for the day: 8 September 2017, whilst another may say that 'th', 'rd' or 'st' should be used. e.g 8th September 2017
Language	A house style may give guidelines about the type of language that should be used in written communication.

 Definition

A template is a pre-prepared electronic document set out using an organisation's house style.

Using templates makes it easier for employees to create business communications that are consistent with the organisation's brand image.

Templates help to save time and reduce errors because common elements are pre-printed and users just have to complete any information that is specific to that particular communication.

In the following example, only the items in bold need to be completed.

 Example

Dear **[customer name]**

Ref: **[Customer Account Number]**

Please find attached your statement of account for **[month]**. The balance outstanding is £ **[balance outstanding]**.

We would appreciate payment by the end of this week. If you have any queries regarding any of the amounts on the statement, please contact me as soon as possible.

Yours sincerely,

Accounts Assistant

4.6 Letter format

Date Line

The date should include the day, the month and the year. The month should always be written in full, e.g. 17 June 2017

Customer Name and Address

The recipient's name and address should be spelt correctly and written on the left hand side of the letter.

Open Salutation

The opening salutation begins with the word 'Dear' and continues with the recipient's title and last name. If you don't know the name of the recipient, you can use 'Dear Sir or Madam'. However, it is better to try to find out the name of the person you are writing to by telephoning the recipient's organisation to ask who you should address the letter to.

Reference

The reference is a short description of the content of the letter.

Body of Letter

The body of the letter should be concise, clear and to the point, and should be divided into paragraphs.

- The first paragraph should state the purpose of the letter.
- The middle paragraph(s) should contain supporting information.
- The final paragraph should state what you would like the recipient to do.

Complimentary close (or closing salutation)

The choice of complimentary close depends on the opening salutation used.

When you know the name of the person you are addressing, e.g. 'Dear Mr or Mrs ...' the closing salutation should be 'Yours sincerely'

If you don't know the addressee's name, and you have used an opening salutation of 'Dear Sir or Madam' the closing salutation should be 'Yours faithfully'

Signature

The letter should be signed above the typed name and job title of the writer.

 Example

                                              Friebe Motors
                                                   Top Lane
                                                  CHEETHAM
                                                   CH5 7TY

                                                17 June 2016

Mr R Moore
Chippendale Lane
CHEETHAM
CH4 8PG

Dear Mr Moore

Re: Cheque Payment of £5,450

Thank you for your cheque payment of £5,450 received today.

Unfortunately, you did not send a remittance advice with the payment so we are not sure which invoices you are paying. Please could you send a remittance advice so that we can make sure that we allocate the payment to the correct invoices?

We look forward to receiving your remittance. In the meantime, if you need any more information please contact me at the above address.

Yours sincerely

D Francis

D Francis
Accounts Administrator

Test your understanding 7

Jodie needs to write a letter to Steven Smart, the Managing Director of one of How Two Ltd's major customers, NB Solutions Ltd.

How should she start the letter? Tick the best option from those provided.

	✓
Hi Steven	
Hello	
Dear Mr Smart	
Dear NB Solutions	

Test your understanding 8

How would you sign off a business letter to someone whose name is not known to you?

	✓
Yours faithfully	
Yours sincerely	
Yours forever	
Kind regards	

Test your understanding 9

For which ONE of the following would a letter seem the most appropriate form of communication?

	✓
Informing staff of the company's performance and a pay rise	
Informing staff of the next training event	
Asking staff for feedback from the previous training event	

Test your understanding 10

Read through the letter shown below and identify TEN errors.

> Morse Manufacturing
> The Old Mill
> Addison Drive
> Newtown
> NW24 8RP

Christopher Barrie

22 Loring Avenue

Little Hinton

Buckinghamshire

HP99 2AQ

Hello Barrie

Ref: 50% discount on all home furnishings

I am pleased to confirm that we have accepted your credit account application.

You're initial credit limit on the account will be £1,500 and you will be required to settle your account within 15 days of purchase.

after a trial period of three months, if payments have been received in a timely fashion, we will discuss your requirements further!

I hope that the above meets with your approval. If I could of been of any more assistance, please let me know.

Otherwise we look forward 2 hearing from you soon.

Yours faithfully,

Kevin Claydon

kevlovesit@hotmail.com

4.7 The use of reports in business

Business reports are used to communicate information formally to internal and external customers.

Reports are used to present a lot of information all together in one document.

4.8   The structure of reports

The format of the report depends on the information being presented but could include:

Title Page	The report will have a front cover or title page which will include: • The name of the person the report is for • The name of the person the report is from • The date of the report.
Summary	A short overview of what can be found in the full report.
Contents page	An index of page numbers where the information can be found.
Introduction	An outline of the report's structure.
Body	The main content of the report which may be sectioned into sub headings.
Conclusion	The main findings from the report.
Appendix	Graphs and charts which support the information in the main report.

Test your understanding 11

Put the following sections of a report into the order in which you would expect to see them. Complete the boxes below using a), b), c) or d).

a) Recommendations	First	
b) Conclusion	Second	
c) Introduction	Third	
d) Appendix	Fourth	

4.9   Instant messaging

This is a useful way of communication within a company since most employees in accounts spend a lot of their working day using a computer. Instant messaging allows an employee to send a message from their computer to anyone within their department. It will immediately appear on the recipient's computer, this means that nobody has to leave their workstation.

5 Verbal communication methods

5.1 Telephone calls

Due to developments in both office and mobile telephone systems, perhaps the most common way for most colleagues to communicate is via telephone. And although much of this communication will be spoken, a text message to a colleague may get a more swift response.

Certain rules for telephone etiquette apply, as is the case for all of the written forms of communication addressed previously. It is vital to remain polite, positive and respectful when speaking on the phone and the appropriate use of language and tone are essential to avoid any misunderstandings.

There are many benefits of telephone conversations with colleagues and customers you know well. For example:

- They are a quick and easy method of instant two-way communication.

- Relating to this, telephone calls give a matter priority. They cannot typically be left for later as e-mails or letters can be due to work prioritisation by the receiver.

- Explanation is also often easier, especially if trying to address more complex issues. A telephone call more easily enables someone to check the other person understands and reword the subject matter if required.

It is important to remain professional when making a business telephone call. Speak clearly, avoid talking too fast. When talking to a customer show respect at all times, call them Sir/Madam/Mr/Mrs/Miss. On occasions they may instruct that you should call them by their first name, if this happens thank them and do as requested. However, if you have cause to contact them again in the future revert back to formality until again or if instructed differently. Avoid using any slang words or abbreviations regardless.

If you are making an internal call to one of your colleagues it may be acceptable to call them by their first name and to not be quite as formal. However, you must remain respectful at all times regardless of the person you may be conversing with, and therefore always use your manners and refrain from swearing.

5.2 Mobile telephones

Due to recent developments in mobile technology, it is now common for most key staff and those with jobs requiring a lot of time out of the office within a company to have business mobile telephones, or more recently, smartphones/tablets.

There are many advantages of increased use of business mobile telephones for a company:

- Staff are now available for more time and without delay

- Meetings can be held virtually and across large geographical areas

- Both customers and colleagues have greater access to the member of staff, allowing better team work and customer care

- The company can monitor phone usage

- Data can be more easily and quickly accessed by staff

- Mobile technology such as text reminders allows new methods of communication with customers.

Just as mobile telephones are more common in a business context, the majority of the population now have a personal device. Most companies will have in place a policy regarding personal calls and the use of mobiles during office hours. Therefore employees may need to sign an 'Acceptable Use' document for both IT and telephones when joining a company.

Using telephones for personal reasons during the working day is typically regarded as unacceptable, except in the case of an emergency or with a manager's permission. Personal calls or internet usage is therefore often restricted to break times. As discussed in the previous chapter, most companies will have a policy in place to specify when personal phone usage is permitted and how/when to utilise company equipment. Usually personal mobile telephones should be switched off in working hours, or at the least on silent mode to not distract the employee or their colleagues.

As well as causing a distraction and preventing productivity, there are also security risks which serve as a reason for these types of restrictions.

Test your understanding 12

The following two statements relate to telephones in business. Tick the boxes to show if they are true or false.

Statement	True	False
It is quicker and easier to communicate with colleagues using e-mail than to do so via telephone.		
Mobile telephones have no place in the workplace as they are only for personal use.		

5.3   Face to face communication and meetings

In addition to communicating with customers and colleagues who are not in the same location as you, there will also be numerous occasions where you will need to communicate face-to-face.

Most of these will be routine conversations in the office, and as such are considered informal communication. The need to be polite and communicate effectively with fellow team members was addressed in the previous chapter.

There will also be occasions when formal face-to-face communication is needed in the workplace. Most of these will be meetings, both with co-workers (for example, departmental staff meetings) and external participants (for example, customer and supplier meetings). Meetings can be both formal and informal and can take place in the office or off-site.

In terms of acceptable behaviour, the courtesy required on the telephone will also apply, however body language (so-called non-verbal communication) is more important.

🔍 Definition

Non-verbal communication refers to the means of communicating in business without using words. Research suggests that up to 80% of communication is through our actions and the signals we show to others. This is commonly known as **body language**.

There are many tips on effective body language in the workplace, but on the whole it is important to appear enthusiastic and interested in what other people say. Using simple tools such as nodding and smiling when others speak and maintaining eye contact will achieve this. It is important not to interrupt others and if you feel the need to disagree or question them to do so in a polite and positive way.

Equally if the person you are talking to starts looking around the room, ensure you pick up on this and change your subject or approach to capture their attention.

5.4   Presentations

Presentations are perhaps the most obvious form of verbal communication. They are typically one person speaking to an audience, with limited interaction or discussion. As such, they provide a great opportunity to express and explain complex messages or brief staff or customers.

Presentations are not just important for managing directors seeking to inspire and inform their staff or salespeople looking to sell products or services to their clients. All parts of a company's business function may need to present their ideas and views to others in a way that their audience will respond to. For accountants, presentations can make an enormous spreadsheet or two hundred page report more digestible for others.

 Test your understanding 13

Rachel works in the accounts department at Hoops & Whoops Ltd, a company providing entertainment for children's parties.

An angry mother calls in to complain about one of the clowns the company use, who had ruined her child's party. She is asking for both an explanation and her money back.

What should Rachel say to the customer? Tick the correct answer.

	✓
With all due respect, that cannot be right. This clown is one of our finest entertainers and has been doing parties for over thirty years. Maybe you should check your facts and call us back?	
I am really sorry to hear that there were issues with the clown at the party, but there is nothing we can do about it now that the party is over. Maybe if you are not happy you should use another supplier next time?	
I am really sorry to hear that there were issues at the party; we take these matters very seriously. We could give you all of your money back if you promise not to ask us any more questions about this.	
I am really sorry to hear that there you were not happy with the clown at the party; we will look into the specific circumstances as we take quality very seriously. We can offer a 10% refund if we find that there was an issue.	

Test your understanding 14

How Two Ltd have been supplying NB Solutions Ltd's with computer and network equipment for a number of years and the account is now worth a substantial amount of money to How Two Ltd.

Otto, the Sales Manager at How Two, feels it would be good to set up a long-term contract with NB Solutions to confirm pricing, discounts and service levels for the future.

Which of the following would be the best way to discuss the future relationship between the two companies and negotiate terms? Tick the most appropriate answer.

	✓
A telephone call	
A face-to-face meeting	
A presentation by Otto	
An e-mail	

6 Spreadsheets and software for workplace communications

6.1 Spreadsheets

Spreadsheets are common tools utilised for accounting functions. They provide a fast and efficient method of presenting and reporting data. Performing calculations are straightforward as there is a formula function that allows the calculation to be done automatically. Spreadsheets can also process and 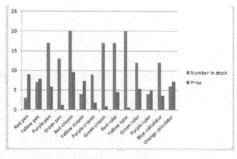 manipulate data, with sorting and filtering among the most common tasks. A spreadsheet allows figures to be presented easily in graphical form which is useful when analysing data such as month on month sales, for example.

When figures and information need to be communicated within the team they are easily transferred through the internal computer system to the relevant department or team member via a spreadsheet, in the format required by the business. Management find them useful to download and take to meetings so that they can refer to the information whenever figures need to be discussed.

6.2 Software for workplace communications

Many of the forms of communication we have detailed in this chapter are enabled by software programs. For example, it is rare for letters to be written by hand and visual aids in presentations tend to come in the form of PowerPoint slides rather than handwritten diagrams or notes.

If we consider the forms of communication described earlier, a corresponding Microsoft Office application will often exist to ensure their accurate and professional delivery. For example:

- Excel is the favoured program for devising spreadsheets. In addition to being able to perform mathematical functions, which are especially useful in accounting, Excel also can present the information in a variety of charts and graphs.

- Word is used for all forms of business writing. A word processing package, it can be used for writing e-mails, the written elements of a report and to type up the minutes of meetings. Spellings, grammar and punctuation can easily be checked and corrected in Word and fonts can be changed to match the most appropriate style.

- Outlook is the program utilised most often for sending e-mails – it also has a calendar feature to assist with time management.

- PowerPoint is the most widely used presentation software, allowing for the production of all aspects of presentations including animations.

Likewise, instant messenger apps may be connected to social media, but also may be connected to an e-mail system. For example, Google provide a chat feature and 'Hangouts' to operate alongside Gmail.

7   Summary and further questions

In this chapter we have identified the different methods of communication in the workplace and the uses of both formal and informal language. You should now be able to identify the best method of communication and the most appropriate software required for any task.

You should be able to manage your time effectively. From the various suggestions in this chapter you may be able to identify which methods are likely to work best for you. You will have learnt how ineffective time manage can have a detrimental effect on other members of the team.

Let us return now to the case study to test your knowledge of these key skills for business.

 Case study activity 10

During the course of a week Jessica is required to communicate using a number of methods of communication. Choose the most appropriate form of communication for Jessica to use for each situation below. Use the pick list provided.

Jessica needs to communicate a lot of information to internal and external customers	
Jessica has received a serious complaint in the post and needs to respond to it	
Jessica has been asked to provide the latest figures from the system for the management to see	
Jessica has been asked to contact a customer and speak to them urgently	
Jessica needs to see a colleague to tell them about some sensitive information	
Jessica has a query that anyone in the department may be able to help with – she needs to contact them all without leaving her desk	

Pick list

Letter	Spreadsheet
Instant messaging	Report
Face-to-face	Telephone

Case study activity 11

Jessica has been asked to write an e-mail to one of How Two Ltd's customers, NB Solutions Ltd, to detail some changes to their account.

It has been agreed that NB Solutions' credit limit will be increased to £30,000 and that weekly statements will be sent via e-mail. An early payment discount of 10% will apply when outstanding invoices are fully paid within 14 days of the goods being received. All deliveries to UK addresses will be free.

Jessica has been asked to contact Dawn-Marie, the Finance Manager at NB Solutions, with whom she has exchanged e-mails in the past.

Complete the e-mail below by selecting the best option from the three provided for each part:

1	Hey D-M	Hi Dawn-Marie	To whom it may concern
2	Further to your recent communications with Otto, I am pleased to confirm some of the new arrangements for your account with us.	Otto has told me to send you an e-mail because he is busy and he knows I have spoken to you before.	I have been asked to contact you as I understand you are not happy with the service How Two Ltd have been providing.
3	I am pleased to confirm that NB Solutions Ltd's credit limit will be increased to £30,000 and we will offer a 10% early payment discount if you pay within 14 days of the invoice dates.	I am pleased to confirm that NB Solutions Ltd's credit limit will be increased to £10,000 and we will offer a 30% early payment discount if you pay within 30 days of the invoice dates.	I am pleased to confirm that due to the fact NB Solutions Ltd is regarded as a very important customer, your credit limit will be increased and we will offer an early payment discount.
4	You will also receive a weekly statement via e-mail to save our postage costs,	You will also receive a weekly statement via e-mail to make sure you pay,	You will also receive a weekly statement via e-mail to keep you informed.
5	I am also pleased to confirm that you will receive a 10% discount on all UK deliveries.	Moving forward I am also pleased to confirm that you will not be charged for UK deliveries.	Due to your complaints, we have reluctantly agreed to not charge you for deliveries to the UK.
6	That should cover everything – sorry if it hasn't.	Please contact me with any queries regarding this.	If you have any queries, please look on our website.
7	Kind regards, Jessica	Yours faithfully, Jessica	Love, J xx

Case study activity 12

Jessica has been asked to select the most appropriate software for each of the following forms of workplace communication.

Use the pick list provided to find the most appropriate software for Jessica to use.

Jessica needs to send a newsletters, adding attachments such as data files and photographs	
Jessica is doing her reports and wants to work out formulas and other figures	
Jessica wants to write a letter and needs help with punctuation, grammar and spelling	
Jessica needs to show what the company does and how it can benefit the customer, to a group of people.	

Pick list

Spreadsheet   E-mail

Word processing   Presentation

Answers to chapter activities

Test your understanding 1

	✓
Jodie should do the straightforward jobs and leave the more difficult ones for her colleagues to complete after she has left for the meeting.	
Jodie should make a list of all that she needs to do in the morning and give each a timescale and priority.	✓
Jodie should realise that it will be difficult to perform all of the tasks so she should put them all off until the next day.	
Jodie should ignore the regional meeting and devote all her time to the tasks she needs to complete in the office.	

Test your understanding 2

Thomas should:

C   Contact his supervisor immediately and explain the problem. He should suggest that he finishes what he considers to be the most urgent task first before starting one of the others.

✎ Test your understanding 3

	Monday	Tuesday	Wednesday	Thursday	Friday
9am - 10am	Check emails	Check emails	Check emails	Check emails	Check emails
10am – 11am	Processing Purchase Orders	Processing Purchase Orders	Processing Purchase Orders	Processing Purchase Orders	Purchase ledger meeting
11am – 12pm	Processing Purchase Orders	Processing Purchase Orders	Processing Purchase Orders	Processing Purchase Orders	Purchase ledger meeting
12pm – 1pm	Checking supplier invoices	Checking supplier invoices	Checking supplier invoices	Checking supplier invoices	Checking supplier invoices
1pm – 2pm	**Lunch**	**Lunch**	**Lunch**	**Lunch**	**Lunch**
2pm – 3pm	Checking supplier invoices	Checking supplier invoices	Checking supplier invoices	Checking supplier invoices	Checking supplier invoices
3pm – 4pm	Supplier account reconciliations	Supplier account reconciliations	Supplier account reconciliations	Purchase Ledger reports	Supplier payment run
4pm – 5pm	Filing documents	Filing documents	Filing documents	Filing documents	Supplier payment run

✎ Test your understanding 4

Decide when you would use these examples of formal or informal language.

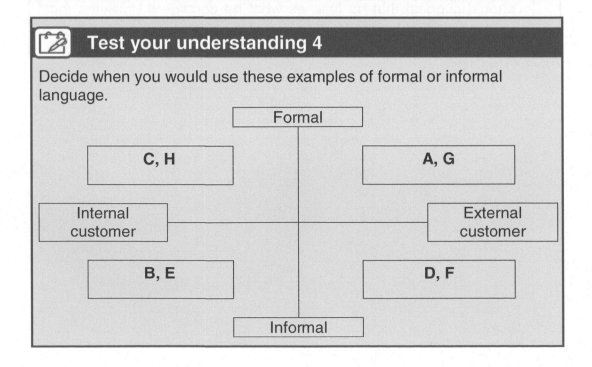

KAPLAN PUBLISHING

Test your understanding 5

	Formal / Informal	Internal / External
A letter to a member of the public responding to a complaint	Formal	External
Asking a colleague whether or not an order has been fulfilled	Informal	Internal
A report for the directors analysing annual business performance	Formal	Internal
A Human Resources policy document for all staff	Formal	Internal
An e-mail to all customers regarding a new invoicing system	Formal	External

Test your understanding 6

	✓
A clear and purposeful subject heading	✓
Slang words	
Simple and well-structured content	✓
Jokes and personal comments	
Capital letters to stress the importance of your thoughts	
An appropriate sign off	✓

Test your understanding 7

	✓
Hi Steven	
Hello	
Dear Mr Smart	✓
Dear NB Solutions	

Test your understanding 8

	✓
Yours faithfully	✓
Yours sincerely	
Yours forever	
Kind regards	

Test your understanding 9

	✓
Informing staff of the company's performance and a pay rise	✓
Informing staff of the next training event	
Asking staff for feedback from the previous training event	

Test your understanding 10

The following errors can be identified:

1. There is no date anywhere on the letter

2. The letter should start 'Dear Mr Barrie'. The salutation of Hello is not appropriate and 'Barrie' is the customer's surname, not first name.

3. The subject of the letter has nothing to do with the content (it is about the opening of a trade account, not discounted furnishings).

4. The second paragraph should start with a capital letter ('After').

5. 'You're' should be 'Your' before credit limit.

6. The second paragraph ends with an exclamation mark which is inappropriate in a business context.

7. In the third paragraph, 'could of' should be 'could have'.

8. In the final sentence the number 2 is used instead of the word 'to'. 'Text speak' is not acceptable in any business communications.

9. As the name of the recipient is known, the letter should end with 'Yours sincerely' rather than 'Yours faithfully'.

10. The writer's signature is inappropriate – there is no job title under the name and the e-mail address provided is not a work e-mail address.

KAPLAN PUBLISHING

Test your understanding 11

First	Introduction (c)
Second	Recommendations (a)
Third	Conclusion (b)
Fourth	Appendix (d)

Test your understanding 12

Statement	True	False
It is quicker and easier to communicate with colleagues using e-mail than to do so via telephone.		✓
Mobile telephones have no place in the workplace as they are only for personal use.		✓

Test your understanding 13

	✓
With all due respect, that cannot be right. This clown is one of our finest entertainers and has been doing parties for over thirty years. Maybe you should check your facts and call us back?	
I am really sorry to hear that there were issues with the clown at the party, but there is nothing we can do about it now that the party is over. Maybe if you are not happy you should use another supplier next time?	
I am really sorry to hear that there were issues at the party, we take these matters very seriously. We could give you all of your money back if you promise not to ask us any more questions about this.	
I am really sorry to hear that there you were not happy with the clown at the party; we will look into the specific circumstances as we take quality very seriously. We can offer a 10% refund if we find that there was an issue.	✓

Test your understanding 14

	✓
A telephone call	
A face-to-face meeting	✓
A presentation by Otto	
An e-mail	

Case study activity 10

Jessica needs to communicate a lot of information to internal and external customers	Report
Jessica has received a serious complaint in the post and needs to respond to it	Letter
Jessica has been asked to provide the latest figures from the system for the management to see	Spreadsheet
Jessica has been asked to contact a customer and speak to them urgently	Telephone
Jessica needs to see a colleague to tell them about some sensitive information	Face-to-face
Jessica has a query that anyone in the department may be able to help with – she needs to contact them all without leaving her desk	Instant messaging

Case study activity 11

1		Hi Dawn-Marie	
2	Further to your recent communications with Otto, I am pleased to confirm some of the new arrangements for your account with us.		
3	I am pleased to confirm that NB Solutions Ltd's credit limit will be increased to £30,000 and we will offer a 10% early payment discount if you pay within 14 days of the invoice dates.		
4			You will also receive a weekly statement via e-mail to keep you informed.
5		Moving forward I am also pleased to confirm that you will not be charged for UK deliveries.	
6		Please contact me with any queries regarding this.	
7	Kind regards, Jessica		

Case study activity 12

Jessica needs to send a newsletters, adding attachments such as data files and photographs	E-mail
Jessica is doing her reports and wants to work out formulas and other figures	Spreadsheet
Jessica wants to write a letter and needs help with punctuation, grammar and spelling	Word processing
Jessica needs to show what the company does and how it can benefit the customer, to a group of people.	Presentation

The principles of sales and purchases

Introduction

The purpose of accounting is to be able to provide financial information about an organisation. For example, managers will want to keep track of the profit made by the organisation in a certain period, and they will also want to see how much the organisation is worth at a specific point in time.

To be able to provide this information it is important to understand the principles of sales and purchases and how these contribute to the profit or loss of a company.

This chapter will introduce you to the accounting terminology used in relation to this.

KNOWLEDGE	CONTENTS
Understand how sales and purchases support business 1.1 Sales and purchases in business 2.1 Understand principles of sales and purchases: sales 2.2 Understand principles of sales and purchases: purchases	1 Income and expenditure 2 Profit and loss 3 Cash and credit transactions 4 Summary and further questions

1 Income and expenditure

1.1 Case study: an introduction

  Case study

Jessica is due to start her first week in the Sales and Purchasing department at How Two Ltd. She is really looking forward to learning how sales and purchases support businesses by monitoring income and expenditure.

Jessica is aware that How Two Ltd is a profit-making organisation. She is therefore keen to learn the principles of sales and purchasing and to be able to identify how they can assist a business to generate more income by means of saving on expenditure.

The purpose of most organisations is to make a profit or to raise funds so that they can continue supplying goods and services to customers. In order to calculate profit, an understanding of income and expenditure is needed.

1.2 What is income?

Any money received from the supply of goods and services to customers is known as income.

1.3 What is expenditure?

Any money paid for purchasing the goods and services and day to day expenses is known as expenditure.

Definitions

Income is the money received by an organisation from selling its goods and services.

Expenditure is the money paid by an organisation to purchase goods and services.

Test your understanding 1

Jessica has been asked to decide which of the following are examples of income and which are examples of expenditure. Tick the correct box.

	Income	Expenditure
Payments to suppliers		
Electricity bill		
The cost of goods and services		
Cash sales		
Sales of services		
Telephone bill		
Water bill		

2 Profit and loss

2.1 What is a profit or loss?

A business needs to make money in order to operate. By selling goods or services they generate income, from this they need to deduct their expenses for buying in those goods and services. This is called the 'profit' or 'loss'.

In order for a business to generate a 'profit', their income needs to be more than their expenses. If their expenses are more than their income, they would make a loss which could make the business fail.

 Definitions

Profit is the amount of money an organisation earns after expenditure has been deducted from income.

Loss is when an organisation has spent more money than it has earned from income.

2.2 What happens when a business makes a profit?

An organisations main goal should be to make a profit. No business can survive long-term if they don't make a profit.

Profit is paid to the owners of a company or its shareholders. Alternatively, it can be used as a saving opportunity to enable the organisation to re-invest and therefore grow the business. Growing a business means expanding it; making it bigger. This may be through investing in research or new technology, opening new offices, operating in new markets or obtaining other businesses. A bigger company means a bigger part of the market share and therefore increased profitability.

2.3 What happens when a business makes a loss?

If a business is spending more on expenses than they are making from the sales of goods or services, they will be making a loss.

If an organisation is making a loss then the chances are that their bank account may become overdrawn. Ultimately, they will be charged high amounts of interest for this which only increases their expenditure even more. If this were to happen, the business may not have enough money to pay their suppliers which could result in the suppliers putting their account on hold, or even withdrawing their credit agreement.

As a result, the business would find it difficult to purchase goods or services for resale, meaning that they would struggle to meet their customer's demands. If this is the case, it can cause problems and the business could fail.

Test your understanding 2

Jessica has been asked to identify which of the following are indicators of a business making a profit or a loss. Put a tick in the correct box.

	Profit	Loss
The business could fail		
The bank account is overdrawn		
A saving opportunity		
There is an opportunity for growth		
There is a high volume of sales		
Money has been invested in new ventures		
Not enough money to pay for purchases		
Suppliers withdraw their credit agreement		

Example

NB Solutions Ltd has recorded all sales income and expenditure for the previous month. Alba, the Accounts Assistant, has been asked to calculate the profit for the month.

	£
Sales income	125,000
Cost of sales	75,000
Wages	15,000
Premises expenses	3,000
Vehicle expenses	2,500

Solution:

To calculate **profit (or loss)** the cost of sales are deducted from the sales income.

	Sales income:	£125,000
−	Cost of sales	- £75,000
−	Wages	- £15,000
−	Premises expenses	- £3,000
−	Vehicle expenses	- £2,500
=	**Total Profit**	**£29,500**

Therefore, Alba can report a profit of £29,500 for the month.

Note: If Alba had ended up with a minus figure at the end of her calculation, she would know that the company had made a loss i.e. NB Solutions Ltd's expenses were more than the company's income.

 Case study

In September, How Two Ltd's Liverpool office had recorded income from sales of £82,000. The cost of those sales was £66,000 and the other expenses were £25,000. Jessica is asked whether the Liverpool office made a profit or a loss.

Solution:

	Sales income:	£82,000
−	Cost of sales	- £66,000
−	Other expenses	- £25,000
	=	-£9,000

Their expenses are more than their income so the Liverpool office of How Two Ltd made a loss of £9,000 in September.

Test your understanding 3

To assess the performance of How Two Ltd's Liverpool office in September, Jessica looks at the figures from the previous month. In August, the Liverpool office recorded income of £85,000. The cost of those sales was £69,000 and the other expenses were £18,000.

Did they make a profit or a loss? How do the two months compare?

 Test your understanding 4

Jessica has been asked to see if the performance of the Liverpool office is similar to the nearest office, in Manchester. The Manchester office of How Two Ltd has recorded all sales income and expenditure for the previous month.

Jessica needs to calculate the profit or loss for the month given the following information:

	£
Sales income from cash and credit sales	78,000
Cost of sales	50,700
Wages	7,500
Premises expenses	1,750
Vehicle expenses	2,000

 Test your understanding 5

Jessica is asked to summarise her findings via e-mail. One of the senior managers asks her a question: If How Two Ltd has total income lower than costs of sales plus expenses, have we made a profit or a loss?

Write a sentence for Jessica to e-mail to the manager to explain the answer to his question.

3 Cash and Credit Transactions

3.1 Customers and clients

Throughout this section, we will refer to customers and clients of a company and the types of transactions in which they are involved.

The term **'customer'** often refers to someone who purchases goods or services from a shop or online. The term **'client'** often refers to someone who is receiving professional services or advice, for example, accountancy services or legal services.

3.2 Recording cash and credit transactions

Income is the amount of money received by an organisation from the sale of its goods or services. Returning to our case study, How Two Ltd sell computers and accessories to their customers; these would be classified as their sales of goods. They also have a help desk that offer advice on technical issues or who deal with broken computers that customers bring into store to be fixed; this would be classified as their sales of services.

Sometimes money from sales is received immediately; this is classified as **cash sales**. At other times, the money is received later; this is classified as **credit sales**. It is important that these cash and credit transactions are recorded separately so that the organisation knows how much money it is owed by customers.

3.3 Cash and credit sales

 Definitions

Sales is the exchange of goods or services to an individual or organisation in exchange for money.

A **customer** is an individual or organisation to whom the goods or services have been sold. The organisation supplying the goods or services will then receive money in exchange.

A **receivable (also known as a debtor)** is a customer who has been sold goods on credit and who owes the business the money in respect of the sale.

Cash Sales is the term used to describe a payment at point of sale. The payment itself can be made by cash (currency), cheque, debit or credit card, or bank transfer. An example of a cash sale is when you go into a shop, choose the items you want to buy, and pay for them immediately.

Credit Sales are sales made where the goods or services will be paid later than the point of sale. Many organisations give credit to their regular trade customers so that one payment can be made for all the transactions made in each month. Credit sales are usually recorded by way of an invoice which will be covered in a later chapter.

3.4 Cash and credit customers

With cash sales the organisation gets the money immediately from the customer and the relationship ends there. With credit customers, there is a risk to the organisation that the customer may not pay for the goods.

Therefore, before allowing customers to pay on credit the organisation will make certain checks to ensure that the customer can pay. If these checks identify that the customer has the ability to pay its debts, payment terms will be agreed with the customer and a credit account set up.

Payment terms usually state the length of time a customer has to pay for their goods and also a maximum amount that they are allowed to owe the business at any one time. The amounts outstanding from customers can be analysed so that a business can see at what point they can expect the money to come into their bank account.

If customers are taking longer to pay than expected, a business should chase for the outstanding monies to ensure a continual flow of cash moving through the organisation.

It is assumed that the money owed by credit customers will be paid and therefore they are classed as **receivables** or **debtors** of the organisation.

Test your understanding 6

Jessica has been asked to identify whether the following would be classified as a cash or credit transaction?

Put a tick in the correct box.

	Cash	Credit
A customer purchases a computer and pays by credit card		
A customer buys a mouse mat, a mouse and a printer and pays by debit card		
A customer buys 5 tablet computers, and pays in 30 days		

3.5 Cash and credit purchases

 Definition

Purchases – to buy goods or services from an organisation in exchange for money.

Cash Purchases are when goods or services are paid for at the time of purchase.

 Case study

How Two Ltd may purchase some stock and pay by 'cash'. Although the payment could be by cash (currency), credit card or debit card or bank transfer, if the payment is made immediately it is classed as a cash purchase.

Credit Purchases are when an organisation pays for the goods or services sometime after making the purchase. The money will be sent to the supplier after an agreed amount of time, for example, thirty days.

The supplier is now a payable of the organisation and as money is owed to the supplier in respect of the transaction.

Definition

A **supplier** is an individual or organisation providing goods or services to another in exchange for money.

A **trade payable** is a supplier who is owed money for goods purchased on credit.

 Test your understanding 7

Jessica has been asked to identify whether the following would be classified as a cash or credit transaction?

Put a tick in the correct box.

	Cash	Credit
The Liverpool office purchases some inventory online and pays by bank transfer		
The London office purchases some inventory and is issued an invoice from the supplier		
The Manchester office purchases a computer and pays by credit card		

Test your understanding 8

Fill in the gaps below to complete the sentences. Choose from the Pick list provided.

When an organisation pays for items of expenditure at the time of purchase this is known as a _____

When an organisation allows a customer to pay the amount they owe at a later date this is known as a _____

Pick List

credit sale   cash sale   cash purchase   credit purchase.

Test your understanding 9

C Froome's Cycle World

Mr Froome has a small shop selling and repairing bicycles for individual customers.

He buys the spare parts that he needs from a large wholesaler.

Do you think that Mr Froome's income comes from cash sales or credit sales?

Do you think that the expenditure for spare parts is cash purchases or credit purchases?

4 Summary and further questions

This chapter has introduced you to some important accounting terminology. You can distinguish between income and expenditure and should also understand that a business needs more income than expenses in order to operate profitably.

We have also looked at the difference between credit sales and purchases and cash sales and purchases. Finally, the chapter looked at how the profit or loss of an organisation is calculated.

Let us now return to the case study for some further practice questions to test your knowledge of this key terminology.

 Case study activity 13

Jessica has been asked to define some key accounts terms to help explain her e-mail to the senior managers. Choose the correct option in each of these statements:

a.   The sum of money spent in making sales is known as [sales/cost of sales]

b.   If total income is greater than the cost of sales plus other expenses the organisation has made a [profit/loss]

c.   If total income is less than the cost of sales plus other expenses the organisation has made a [profit/loss]

Case study activity 14

Jessica needs to decide whether the following How Two Ltd transactions are cash or credit sales, or cash or credit purchases? Put a tick in the correct box.

	Cash Sale	Credit Sale	Cash Purchase	Credit Purchase
Printer paper bought from a supplier and paid for immediately.				
Cables delivered to a customer who will pay at the end of the month.				
Laptop components bought from a supplier on credit.				
A payment received from a customer for goods purchased online and paid for at the checkout.				

 Case study activity 15

Last month How Two Ltd's Head Office recorded income and expenditure in the table below:

Income and Expenditure	£
Sales	156,000
Cost of Sales	93,600
Wages	21,060
Administration Expenses	18,720
Selling Expenses	12,844

Jessica needs to use the income and expenditure figures to calculate the profit or loss and state underneath whether this would be a profit or loss.

Profit / Loss: £

Case study activity 16

The following month's recorded income and expenditure is shown in the table below:

Income and Expenditure	£
Sales	152,880
Cost of Sales	91,728
Wages	20,640
Administration Expenses	18,350
Selling Expenses	12,590

Jessica needs to use the income and expenditure figures to calculate the profit or loss and state underneath whether this would be a profit or loss.

Profit / Loss: £

Answers to chapter activities

Test your understanding 1

	Income	Expenditure
Payments to suppliers		✓
Electricity bill		✓
The cost of goods and services		✓
Cash sales	✓	
Sales of services	✓	
Telephone bill		✓
Water bill		✓

Test your understanding 2

	Profit	Loss
The business could fail		✓
The bank account is overdrawn		✓
A saving opportunity	✓	
There is an opportunity for growth	✓	
There is a high volume of sales	✓	
Money has been invested in new ventures	✓	
Not enough money to pay for purchases		✓
Suppliers withdraw their credit agreement		✓

Test your understanding 3

	£
Sales income	85,000
Cost of sales	-69,000
Other expenses	-18,000
	-2,000

This means that their sales income is lower than their expenses and therefore they have made **a loss of £2,000**.

Although this is a loss, it is £7,000 less than the loss in September.

Test your understanding 4

	£
Sales income	78,000
Cost of sales	-50,700
Wages	-7,500
Premises expenses	-1,750
Vehicle expenses	-2,000
	16,050

The company have made **a profit of £16,050** because their sales income is more than the total of their expenditure.

Test your understanding 5

As their sales income is lower than cost of sales plus expenses, the business has made a loss.

Test your understanding 6

	Cash	Credit
A customer purchases a computer and pays by credit card	✓	
A customer buys a mouse mat, a mouse and a printer and pays by debit card	✓	
A customer buys 5 tablet computers, and pays in 30 days		✓

Test your understanding 7

	Cash	Credit
The Liverpool office purchases some inventory online and pays by bank transfer	✓	
The London office purchases some inventory and is issued an invoice from the supplier		✓
The Manchester office purchases a computer and pays by credit card	✓	

 Test your understanding 8

When an organisation pays for items of expenditure at the time of purchase this is known as a **cash purchase.**

When an organisation allows a customer to pay the amount they owe at a later date this is known as a **credit sale.**

 Test your understanding 9

Mr Froome's income is most likely to be from cash sales. His customers are individuals who will probably pay when they come to pick up their bicycles. They are unlikely to be very regular customers.

His expenditure for the spare parts is likely to be a credit purchase. As Mr Froome will buy regularly from the supplier he may have been given credit so that he can make daily or weekly purchases and then pay for all he owes at a later date.

 Case study activity 13

a.   The sum of money spent in making sales is known as **cost of sales**

b.   If total income is greater than the cost of sales plus other expenses the organisation has made a **profit**

c.   If total income is less than the cost of sales plus other expenses the organisation has made a **loss**

Case study activity 14

	Cash Sale	Credit Sale	Cash Purchase	Credit Purchase
Printer paper bought from a supplier and paid for immediately.			✓	
Cables delivered to a customer who will pay at the end of the month.		✓		
Laptop components bought from a supplier on credit.				✓
A payment received from a customer for goods purchased online and paid for at the checkout.	✓			

Case study activity 15

	£
Sales	156,000
Cost of Sales	-93,600
Wages	-21,060
Administration Expenses	-18,720
Selling Expenses	-12,844
	9,776

Profit / Loss: £ 9,776 Profit

Case study activity 16

	£
Sales	152,880
Cost of Sales	-91,728
Wages	-20,640
Administration Expenses	-18,350
Selling Expenses	-12,590
	9,572

Profit / Loss: £9,572 Profit

Business documentation

7

Introduction

It is important that customer and supplier transactions are recorded separately so that organisations know how much money they are owed by customers, and how much they owe to suppliers.

Business documents are used to record these transactions and the documents are exchanged between the supplier and the customer so that both parties have a record of each transaction. It is important that both the supplier and the customer keep a copy of each of these documents. Mistakes can happen and each document is proof of each stage of the transaction.

The name of a document will depend on whether we look at it from the point of view of the seller or the purchaser. Thus an invoice may be called a 'sales invoice' for the seller but a 'purchase invoice' for the purchaser, although it is the same document.

KNOWLEDGE	CONTENTS
Understand how sales and purchases support business	1 Sales documentation
2.1 Sales	2 Purchases documentation
2.2 Purchases	3 Summary and further questions
2.3 Payment terms	
Apply business procedures to sales and purchases	
3.1 Business procedures for sales and procedures	

1 Sales documentation

1.1 Case study: an introduction

 Case study

Jessica has really enjoyed her induction and feels like she is getting used to the terminology used within her department. She understands the principles behind sales and purchases and has now been tasked with looking through the different types of business documentation that she will come across on a day to day basis.

She is going to be shown what information is required on each document and then she will then be given the opportunity of completing some of these herself to be checked by her manager.

1.2 Offering credit and price quotations

Most transactions between business organisations will be on credit terms and this involves an element of risk. The goods are being taken away or delivered to the customer now with the promise of payment in the future. Therefore, suppliers must be confident that payment will be received.

In some organisations it is common practice to quote prices to customers over the telephone particularly if there is a catalogue or price list from which there are no deviations in price. However, some businesses will be prepared to offer certain customers goods at different prices and discounts may be offered and/or given to customers. Therefore, it is often the case that a price quotation is sent to a customer showing the price at which the goods that they want can be bought. The customer can then decide whether or not to buy the goods at that price. If they decide to purchase the goods upon receipt of the quotation, this can be used to generate the sales invoice later on in the sales process.

1.3 Purchase Order

If the customer is happy with the price quotation that they have received from the supplier then they will complete a purchase order for the goods or services required and send it to their supplier.

This document will state the details of the goods required, including:

- the quantity and description of the goods
- the price and other terms
- the supplier's code number for the items
- the date the order was placed.

When the supplier receives a purchase order, it is important for them to check all of the details carefully as it forms part of the sales contract.

- Is the price the same as the one which was quoted to the customer?
- Are the delivery terms acceptable?
- Are any discounts applicable?

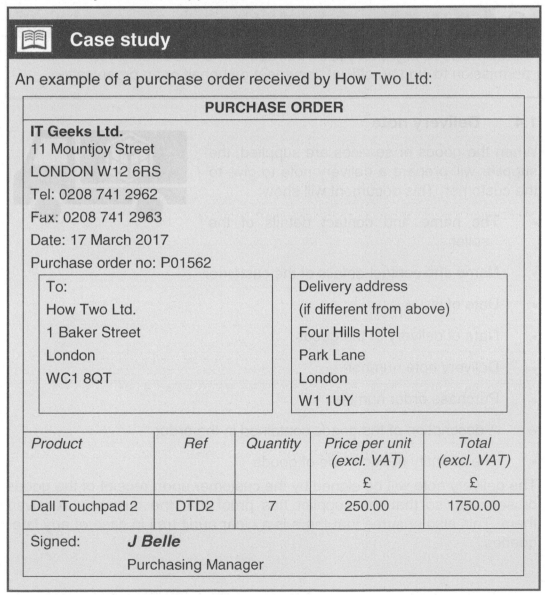

📖 Case study

An example of a purchase order received by How Two Ltd:

PURCHASE ORDER

IT Geeks Ltd.
11 Mountjoy Street
LONDON W12 6RS
Tel: 0208 741 2962
Fax: 0208 741 2963
Date: 17 March 2017
Purchase order no: P01562

To:	Delivery address
How Two Ltd.	(if different from above)
1 Baker Street	Four Hills Hotel
London	Park Lane
WC1 8QT	London
	W1 1UY

Product	Ref	Quantity	Price per unit (excl. VAT) £	Total (excl. VAT) £
Dall Touchpad 2	DTD2	7	250.00	1750.00

Signed: *J Belle*
             Purchasing Manager

Notes:

a) The customer, IT Geeks Ltd. has placed an order with the supplier of computers, How Two Ltd.

b) The purchase order clearly states that the customer wants to purchase 7 Dall Touch Pad 2's at a price of £250.00 each.

c) The total amount that the customer wants to pay for the tablet computers is £1,750.00 (7 touchpads x £250.00 = £1,750.00).

d) If How Two Ltd. do not agree with any of these details, they will need to contact IT Geeks Ltd. immediately. The purchase order has been signed by J Belle, the authorised signatory. This is important to demonstrate that the process has been completed as required by the business.

 Definition

An **authorised signatory** is an individual who has been given permission to sign an official document on behalf of an organisation.

1.4   Delivery note

When the goods or services are supplied, the supplier will prepare a delivery note to give to the customer. This document will show:

*   The name and contact details of the seller

*   Name and contact details of the customer

*   Date of issue

*   Date of delivery of the goods

*   Delivery note number

*   Purchase order number

*   A description of the goods contained in the order

*   The quantity of each type of goods

The delivery note will be signed by the customer upon receipt of the goods or services, so that the supplier has proof that the customer received them. This also ensures that there is a clear audit trail in case of any later queries.

1.5 The sales invoice

After the goods have been delivered, the supplier will request payment from the customer by sending an invoice. The invoice will state the code, quantity, description and price of the goods. The invoice will also have a sequential number so that it can be filed in order. The documentation used in order to generate this would include the quotation if there is one, a price list if it's a standard invoice and the delivery note.

 Case study

An example of a sales invoice provided by How Two Ltd:

INVOICE

How Two Ltd.

1 Baker Street
London
WC1 8QT
Tel: 020 7890 1234
Fax: 020 7890 1235

Invoice no: 005673
Tax point: 25 March 2017
VAT reg no: 618 2201 63
Delivery note: DN00673
Account no: BEL65

To:	**Delivery:**	**Delivery date:**
IT Geeks Ltd.	Four Hills Hotel	25 March 2017
11 Mountjoy St	Park Lane	
London W12 6RS	London W1 1UY	

Date: 25 March 2017   **Sales order number:** 41161

Product	Quantity	Price per unit (£)	Total (£)
Dall Touchpad 2	7	250.00	1,750.00
		VAT 20%	350.00
		Total	2,100.00
Payment terms: 14 days net			

Notes:

This invoice confirms the price of the goods supplied to the customer

a) 7 Dall Touchpad 2's which have been supplied to the IT Geeks Ltd.

b) The price for the goods is £1,750.00

c) Value Added Tax (VAT) of 20%, £350.00 has been added to the cost of the goods.

d) The amount of £2,100.00 is now due from the customer.

e) The payment is due in 14 days from the date of the invoice.

1.6 Pricing and discounts

Unit prices for goods or services are kept in master files which must be updated regularly. If a price quotation has been sent to a customer then this must be used to determine the price to use on the invoice.

Trade discounts are a definite amount that is deducted from the list price of the goods for the supplies to some customers, with the intention of encouraging and rewarding customer loyalty. As well as checking the actual calculation of the trade discount on the face of the invoice, the supplier's file or the price quotation should be checked to ensure that the correct percentage of trade discount has been deducted.

Even if no trade discount appears on the purchase invoice, the supplier's file or price quotation must still be checked as it may be that a trade discount should have been deducted.

A **bulk discount** is similar to a trade discount in that it is deducted from the list price on the invoice. However, a bulk discount is given by a supplier for orders above a certain size.

A **prompt payment discount** is offered to customers if they settle the invoice within a certain time period. The discount is expressed as a percentage of the invoice total but is not deducted from the invoice total as it is not certain whether or not it will be accepted. Instead the details of the settlement discount will be noted at the bottom of the invoice.

Test your understanding 1

Match the transaction to the relevant document:

Transaction	Document
A document sent by the supplier to the customer listing the goods or services supplied and requesting payment	Purchase Order
A document sent to a supplier detailing the goods that the customer wants to purchase.	Invoice
A document sent to a customer to accompany the goods. The customer signs this upon receipt of their items.	Delivery Note

1.7 VAT (sales tax)

VAT (Value Added Tax) also known as Sales Tax, is collected on behalf of HMRC (Her Majesty's Revenue and Customs) by companies in the UK. VAT registered companies charge VAT on the supply of goods and services to their customers. They can claim back any VAT paid on their purchases. The amount that gets paid to HMRC is the total amount of VAT charged to their customers minus the total amount of VAT that they can claim back on their purchases.

 Definitions

Sales tax (VAT) is charged on the **taxable supply of goods and services** in the United Kingdom by a **taxable person** in the course of a business carried on by him.

Output tax is the tax charged on the sale of goods and services.

Input tax is the tax paid on the purchase of goods and services.

1.8 Rates of VAT (sales tax)

Taxable supply is the supply of all items except those which are **exempt.** Examples of exempt items are as follows:

• certain land and buildings, where sold, leased or hired

• insurance

• postal services

Input tax cannot be reclaimed where the trader's supplies are all exempt.

There are three rates of sales tax (VAT in the UK) on taxable supplies:

1.   Some items are 'zero-rated' (similar to exempt except that input tax can be reclaimed), examples of which include:

- water and most types of food

- books and newspapers

- drugs and medicines

- children's clothing and footwear.

2.   There is a special rate of 5% for domestic fuel and power

3.   All other items are rated at the standard rate of 20%.

For the purpose of this assessment, you will normally be dealing with taxable supplies at the standard rate of 20%.

Therefore, if you are given the net price of goods, the price excluding VAT, then the amount of VAT is 20% or 20/100 of this price.

Note: VAT is always rounded down to the nearest penny.

 Example

A sale is made for £360.48 plus VAT. What is the amount of VAT to be charged on this sale?

Solution

VAT = £360.48 × 20/100 = £72.09

Remember to round down to the nearest penny.

An alternative way of calculating this would to be to multiply the net amount of £360.48 by 20% = £72.09.

If a price is given that already includes the VAT then calculating the VAT requires an understanding of the price structure where VAT is concerned.

	%
Selling price excl. VAT (net)	100
VAT	20
	———
Selling price incl. VAT (gross)	120
	———

KAPLAN PUBLISHING

Example

How Two Ltd offer a small office starter pack, with a selling price of £3,000 **inclusive** of VAT. What is the VAT on the goods and the net price of these goods?

Solution

	£
Net price (£3,000 ÷ 120 x 100)	2,500
VAT (£3,000 ÷ 120 x 20)	500
Gross price	3,000

 Test your understanding 2

Calculate the net, VAT and gross figures for the following transactions:

a)　A credit sale for £3,600 inclusive of VAT

b)　A cash sale for £2,800 exclusive of VAT

	a) Credit Sale	b) Cash Sale
Net		
VAT		
Gross		

 Test your understanding 3

Alba works in the accounts office at NB Solutions Ltd. She has been asked to check three invoices relating to office supplies.

Invoice 1 – NB Solutions purchased 24 boxes of paper towels at £12.45 for each box. What is the total cost of the paper towels?

Invoice 2 – NB Solutions spent £250 excluding (or net of) VAT on stationery. How much VAT would be charged?

Invoice 3 – NB Solutions bought two new dishwashers for the staff kitchens, at a total cost of £480 including VAT. How much VAT would have been included in the cost?

1.9   Preparing a sales invoice

 Case study

Dave Woody is the sales invoicing clerk for How Two Ltd, a VAT registered IT and Computer Consumables company.

Dave prepares the sales invoices to be sent to the customer from the price list and a copy of the delivery note sent up to him by the sales department.

Today he has received the following delivery note from the sales department:

How Two Ltd.

Delivery note: 1036
Date of issue: 30th October 20X7
Purchase order number: PO1612

To: IT Crowd PLC.   **From: How Two Ltd.**
   19 Bond Street   1 Baker Street
   Chichester   London
   CH1 6MT   WC1 8QT

Delivery Address:
As Above

Delivery date: 31st October 20X7

Quantity	Code	DESCRIPTION	Size
10	CJA 991	Codie Laptop	12"
15	CJA 992	Codie Laptop	14"
5	CJA 994	Codie Laptop	15.7"

Received by: ....

Signature: .... Date: ....

Code	Description	Screen Size	Unit price	VAT rate
CJA 991	Codie Laptop	12"	249.00	Standard
CJA 992	Codie Laptop	14"	279.00	Standard
CJA 993	Codie Laptop	15"	319.00	Standard
CJA 994	Codie Laptop	15.7"	349.00	Standard

The customer file shows that IT Crowd PLC's account number is ITC 4125 and that a trade discount of 10% is offered to this customer.

Dave must now prepare the sales invoice. Today's date is 2nd November 20X7 and the last invoice issued was numbered 95123.

Solution

INVOICE

How Two Ltd.

Invoice to:
IT Crowd PLC.
19 Bond Street
Chichester
CH1 6MT

How Two Ltd
1 Baker Street
London
WC1 8QT

Tel: 0207 890 1234
Fax: 0207 890 1235

Deliver to:

As above

Invoice no: 95124
Tax point: 2nd November 17
VAT reg no: 618 2201 63
Delivery note no: 1036
Account no: ICT 4125

Code	Description	Quantity	VAT rate	Unit price	Amount net of VAT
			%	£	£
CJA 991	**Codie Laptop**	10	20	249.00	2,490.00
CJA 992	**Codie Laptop**	15	20	279.00	4,185.00
CJA 994	**Codie Laptop**	5	20	349.00	1,745.00
					8,420.00
Trade discount 10%					(842.00)
					7,578.00
VAT					1,515.60
Total amount payable					9,093.60

How did Dave do it?

Step 1 Enter today's date on the invoice and the invoice number which should be the next number after the last sales invoice number.

Step 2 Enter the customer details – name, address and account number.

Step 3 Refer now to the delivery note copy and enter the delivery note number and the quantities, codes and descriptions of the goods.

Step 4 Refer to the price list and enter the unit prices of the goods and the rate of VAT

Step 5 Now for the calculations – firstly multiply the number of each item by the unit price to find the VAT exclusive price – then total these total prices – finally calculate the trade discount as 10% of this total, £8,420.00 × 10% = £842.00 and deduct it.

Step 6 Calculate the VAT – in this case there is only standard rate VAT on the laptops but you must remember to deduct the trade discount (£8,420 – £842) before calculating the VAT amount £7,578 × 20% = £1,515.60 – add the VAT to the invoice total after deducting the trade discount.

Test your understanding 4

As part of her role at How Two Ltd, Jessica is required to generate sales invoices.

Today she has received the following delivery note from the sales department.

Delivery Note

How Two Ltd.

To: St Peter's Secondary School
191 St. Petersgate
Manchester
M2 6KS

From: How Two Ltd.
1 Baker Street
London
WC1 8QT

Delivery Address:
As Above

Delivery note: 1114
Date of issue: 30th October 20X7
Purchase order number: P6486

Delivery date: 31st October 20X7

Quantity	Code	DESCRIPTION	Size
5	SMG 121	Samsong HD Monitor	17"
12	SMG 123	Samsong HD Monitor	24"
8	SMG 124	Samsong HD Monitor	28"

Received by: ....

Signature: .... Date: ....

Code	Description	Screen Size	Unit price	VAT rate
SMG 121	Samsong HD Monitor	17"	69.99	Standard
SMG 122	Samsong HD Monitor	19"	99.99	Standard
SMG 123	Samsong HD Monitor	24"	129.99	Standard
SMG 124	Samsong HD Monitor	28"	149.99	Standard

The customer file shows that St. Peter's Secondary School's account number is SPS 1124 and that a bulk discount of 15% is offered to this customer.

She must now prepare the sales invoice and pass it back to Dave Woody to be checked. Today's date is 3rd November 20X7 and the last invoice issued was numbered 95156.

Solution

INVOICE

How Two Ltd.

Invoice to:

Deliver to:

How Two Ltd
1 Baker Street
London
WC1 8QT

Tel: 0207 890 1234
Fax: 0207 890 1235

Invoice no:
Tax point:
VAT reg no:
Delivery note no:
Account no:

Code	Description	Quantity	VAT rate	Unit price	Amount net of VAT
			%	£	£
SMG 121					
SMG 123					
SMG 124					
Bulk discount					
VAT					
Total amount payable					

Test your understanding 5

You work for Cavalier Beds as a sales invoicing clerk. Your task is to prepare a sales invoice for each customer using the information below.

Today is 28 October, 20X6 and you have received the following delivery note from the sales department.

Use the information from the delivery note, the information from the customer file and the price list below to prepare an invoice for KP Furniture Ltd.

The last invoice issued was Invoice No. 67894.

Delivery Note:

Delivery note: 6785

To: KP Furniture Ltd   **Cavalier Beds**
9 Paris Street   **3 Brussels Road**
COLCHESTER   **County Road**
CF25 1XY   **Gloucester**
                     GL6 6TH
                     Tel: 01456 698271
                     Fax: 01456 698272

Delivery date: 27 October 20X6

Quantity	Code	DESCRIPTION	Size
5	MAT15K	Deluxe Mattress	King Size

Received by: ....

Signature: .... Date: ....

Customer File:

The customer file shows that KP Furniture Ltd's account number is KP12 and a trade discount of 10% is offered to this customer.

Price List:

Code	Description	Size	Unit price	VAT rate
MAT15S	Deluxe Mattress	Single	58.00	Standard
MAT15D	Deluxe Mattress	Double	74.00	Standard
MAT15K	Deluxe Mattress	King	98.00	Standard

Cavalier Beds
3 Brussels Road
County Road
Gloucester
GL6 6TH
Tel: 01456 698271   Fax: 01456 698272

Invoice to:

Invoice no:

Date:

VAT reg no: 488 7922 26

Delivery note
no:

Account no:

Code		Quantity	VAT rate	Unit price £	Amount excl of VAT £
			20%	£	
Trade discount 10%					
Subtotal					
VAT					
Total amount payable					

1.10 The sales day book (SDB)

The sales day book records individual invoices issued to credit customers within one day, week or month. It is basically a list which is totalled at the end of the specified period to indicate how much a company has made in sales, how much VAT they owe to HMRC in respect of those sales and how much they are owed in total by their customers. It will then be used to perform double entry bookkeeping, which you will learn about in the AAT Foundation Certificate.

Example

SALES DAY BOOK

Date	Customer	Reference	Invoice number	Total £	VAT £	Sales £
1 July	Althams Ltd	ALT01	45787	120.00	20.00	100.00
2 July	Broadhurst plc	BRO02	45788	240.00	40.00	200.00
			TOTALS	360.00	60.00	300.00

Notes

- The reference number is the code number of the customer's account in the sales ledger this information can be found on the invoice.
- The invoice number is the number of the invoice issued for each sale.
- The Sales column is the total value of the goods sold as shown on the invoice after deducting trade discount, i.e. net of VAT.
- The amount of VAT is recorded in a separate column to show the amount owing to HMRC for these invoices.
- The Total column shows the total amount due from credit customers (Receivables).

2 Purchases

2.1 Payment terms

As mentioned previously, the majority of business transactions nowadays are conducted on credit terms. This applies to both sales and purchases.

When a credit account is set up with a supplier an agreement is put in place which states the point at which payment is to be made for goods and services, any conditions of payment and any discounts that may be applicable. This helps to ensure that suppliers are paid on time and to give them an idea of cash flows within the business i.e. at what point they can expect the money to come into their bank account.

Payment in advance

A payment in advance is where a payment for goods or services is made ahead of schedule. This is not uncommon when dealing with larger orders as it helps the supplier to cover any 'out of pocket' expenses or to pay for the materials required to produce the order if they don't have enough capital to fund the purchase.

A payment in advance also helps safeguard the supplier against customers who don't pay or those that cancel a large order at the last minute.

 Example – payment in advance

Where a supplier requests a 50% upfront payment from the buyer.

Payment on delivery

Payment on delivery is where the supplier will distribute goods to the customer and take payment for the goods upon delivery. If the customer does not pay for the goods, they are returned to the supplier.

Payment after invoice date

A payment after the invoice date gives the customer a certain number of calendar days to make payment 'after' the date of the invoice. The supplier can specify how many days this would be but quite commonly this is 10, 14, 30 or 60 days after the invoice date. This arrangement would be put in place as part of the supplier agreement.

Payment at the end of the month of invoice

A payment at the end of the month of invoice means that the supplier is expecting the money at the end of the month in which they have issued the invoice.

 Example – payment at the end of month

Where an invoice is issued on the 15th September, the supplier will be expecting payment by the 30th September.

2.2 The Purchasing Process

The flow chart on the following page demonstrates the process that How Two Ltd would follow when making a purchase.

Case study

How Two Ltd select a supplier

Some businesses will have an **approved supplier list**. This is a list of suppliers who are reliable and have the capacity to meet their customers needs. An approved supplier usually provides a consistent high level of service along with excellent quality standards of their products.

They then raise a purchase order and send to the supplier

The purchase order in the purchasing process is exactly the same as that in the sales process. The only difference is that we are effectively the customer and therefore we are the ones completing the document and sending it to the supplier.

How Two Ltd receive the goods or services from the supplier

How Two Ltd check the delivery note against the goods received and sign the delivery note to say that they agree that it matches

The delivery note contains details as stated in the Sales section above. If there are any differences between the delivery note and the goods received, How Two Ltd. makes a note of any differences and queries them with the supplier. This would be noted before the delivery note was signed because otherwise How Two Ltd. could be invoiced for goods that they have never actually received.

How Two Ltd complete a goods received note (GRN)

A **goods received note** is an internal document used to identify proof of goods actually received. See below for further explanation.

How Two Ltd receive an invoice from the supplier in respect of the purchase

How Two Ltd check the invoice received from the supplier against the purchase order, delivery note/goods received note to ensure that they have been invoice correctly

Once satisfied that they have been invoiced accurately for their purchase, How Two Ltd make a payment to the supplier and record the expenditure.

2.3   The Goods Received Note (GRN)

A goods received note is an internal document that is used to document the receipt of goods or services. Upon delivery, the goods received will be checked against the delivery note sent from the supplier. If everything is present and correct, the customer will sign the delivery note to be returned to the supplier and will generate a GRN as proof of what has been received. This is then compared to the purchase order and the supplier invoice before payment is made.

 Case study

You work for How Two Ltd. and have been asked to prepare a goods received note using the following information:

Today is 31st October 20X7, there has been a delivery of goods into the warehouse. Yacob Solvez has checked the goods received and agrees that the details on the following delivery note are correct.

Using the information in the delivery note below, prepare the goods received note as requested, ensuring all of the relevant details are entered.

Delivery Note	
To: How Two Ltd. 1 Baker Street London WC1 8QT	**From: PC's R Us Ltd.** 212 Wellington Street London WC12 8RD

Delivery Address:
1 Baker Street
London
WC1 8QT

Delivery note: 1056
Date of issue: 30th October 20X7
Purchase order number: PO5571

Delivery date: 31st October 20X7

Quantity	Code	DESCRIPTION
20	DKT476	Dall Laptop Model SKW665
25	ESMJA2	Epsan MJA2 projectors

Received by: ....

Signature: ....   Date: ....

Goods Received Note

Goods Received Note

Received From:
PC's R Us
212 Wellington Street
London
WC12 8RD

GRN number: 102

Date goods received: 31st October 20X7

Delivery note number: 1056

Quantity	Code	DESCRIPTION
20	DKT476	Dall Laptop Model SKW665
25	ESMJA2	Epsan MJA2 projectors

Received by: *YACOB SOLVEZ*...

Signature: *Y. Solvez*................. Date: *31st October 2017*..........

Note:

The details entered include the dates that the goods have been received, a goods received note number, the delivery note number from the supplier (so that it can be matched up later), the supplier details, quantities, descriptions and codes of the goods received and then details of the person who has received the goods into store.

 Test your understanding 6

Jessica has been asked to prepare a goods received note using the following information:

Today is 31st October 20X7, there has been a delivery of goods into the warehouse.

Jessica has checked the goods received and agree that the details on the following delivery note are correct.

The last GRN created was number 123.

Delivery Note:

Delivery Note		
Delivery note: 2212		
Date of issue: 30th October 20X7		
Purchase order number: PO5589		

To: How Two Ltd.   From: Tablet World
   1 Baker Street   477 High Street
   London   Oxford
   WC1 8QT   OX10 5WD

Delivery Address:
1 Baker Street
London
WC1 8QT

Delivery date: 31st October 20X7

Quantity	Code	DESCRIPTION
15	SSX52	Samsong SX52 9" Tablet computers
15	DL656	Dall MC656 8" Tablet computers

Received by: ....

Signature: .... Date: ....

Goods Received Note:

Goods Received Note		
Received From:		

GRN number:
Date goods received:
Delivery note number:

Quantity	Code	DESCRIPTION

Received by:...

Signature: .... Date: ....

2.4 The purchases day book

As seen earlier in the chapter, credit sales are recorded in the 'sales day book'. In the case of credit purchases, we have the 'purchases day book'.

The purchases day book is simply a list of the purchases invoices that are to be processed for a given period (e.g. a week). In its simplest form, the purchases day book will comprise just the names of the suppliers and the amount of the invoices received in the week.

Example

PURCHASES DAY BOOK

Date	Supplier	Reference	Invoice number	Total £	VAT £	Purchases £
1 Sept 17	W E L Ltd	Q73243	56712	1,800	300	1,500
3 Sept 17	Vivalitee plc	L73244	AV942	402	67	335
			TOTALS	2,202	367	1,835

Example

You work in the accounts department of R Porte Manufacturing Ltd and have received the following:

R Moore Fashions

12 Dutch Corner
High Wycombe
HG4 7NQ

Invoice no: 005673
Tax point: 14 July 2016

INVOICE

To: R Porte Manufacturing Ltd
   5 Ventoux Crescent, Cardiff, CA2 3HU

Product	Quantity	Price per unit £	Total £
Cargo pants	5	25.00	125.00
T-shirts	10	15.00	150.00
			275.00
		VAT 20%	55.00
		Total	330.00
Payment terms: 30 days net			

As you are dealing with documents for R Porte Manufacturing and this invoice is sent to you at R Porte Manufacturing, R Moore Fashions must be the supplier Therefore, this is a supplier invoice and should be entered into the **purchases day book.**

The entry would appear as follows:

Date	Supplier	Reference	Invoice number	Total £	VAT £	Purchases £
14 July 16	R Moore Fashions	MORS78	005673	330	55	275
			TOTALS	330	55	275

3 Summary and further questions

In this chapter we have looked in detail at the documents used to record transactions for credit and cash customers. You should now know what information is required for each of these documents and you should be able to accurately generate them from given information.

Let us return to the case study to see how Jessica uses some of the documents to record sales and purchases at How Two Ltd.

 Case study activity 17

Jessica has been given three pieces of paper:

- A delivery note
- A sales invoice
- A purchase order

Match the document with the correct description to help Jessica understand how they relate to sales or purchases.

	Document
Sent by the customer (How Two Ltd) to state which goods they want to purchase	
Sent by the supplier to How Two Ltd with the goods when despatched	
Sent by the supplier to How Two Ltd to inform them of how much the goods cost	

Case study activity 18

Jessica has been asked to prepare a delivery note using the information below:

Today is 29th October 20X7 and the following purchase order has been processed with the goods ready to be despatched to the customer. The last delivery note issued was number 1026 and the goods are due to be delivered tomorrow.

Using the information above along with the purchase order below, prepare the delivery note as requested, ensuring all of the relevant details are entered.

PURCHASE ORDER

Redshaw Cables
17 High Street
Manchester M1 6RS
Tel: 0161 741 2962
Fax: 0161 741 2963
Date: 23rd October 20X7
Purchase order no: P01562

To:	Delivery address
How Two Ltd.	(if different from above)
1 Baker Street	Four Lane Ends
London	New Mills
WC1 8QT	SK22 4LG

Product	Ref	Quantity	Price per unit (excl. VAT) £	Total (excl. VAT) £
HDMI Cables	HDMI62	20	15.00	300.00
Epsan SXA projectors	ESXA14	5	300.00	1,500.00
Signed:	J Johnson Purchasing Manager			

Delivery Note:

Delivery Note

To: **From:**

Delivery Address:

Delivery note:
Date of issue:
Purchase order number:

Delivery date:

Quantity	Code	DESCRIPTION

Received by: ....

Signature: .... Date: ....

Case study activity 19

Jessica has been asked to enter the invoice below into the sales day book.

How Two Ltd			
1 Baker Street London WC1 8QT		Invoice no: 5698 Tax point: 26 Nov 2017	

INVOICE

To: G Thomas (A/C Ref TH02)
5 Holland Crescent, Chesham CA2 3HU

Product	Quantity	Price per unit	Total
Goods (Deluxe Laptop Case)	5	£50.12	£250.60
		VAT 20%	£50.12
		Total	£300.72
Payment terms: 30 days net			

Complete the Sales Day Book below with the correct information:

_Date	Customer	Reference	Invoice No	Total £	VAT £	Net £

 Case study activity 20

Given the document below should Jessica record it in the sales day book or the purchases day book or both?

King & Co			
Highbrow HI4 3SQ		Invoice no: 2867 Tax point: 18 June 20X6	

Invoice

To: How Two Ltd
1 Baker Street, London WC1 8QT

Product	Quantity	Price per unit	Total
Item 5	10	£35.50	£355.00
		VAT 20%	£71.00
		Total	£426.00
Payment terms: 15 days net			

Answers to chapter activities

Test your understanding 1

Transaction	Document
A document sent by the supplier to the customer listing the goods or services supplied and requesting payment	Purchase Order
A document sent to a supplier detailing the goods that the customer wants to purchase.	Invoice
A document sent to a customer to accompany the goods. The customer signs this upon receipt of their items.	Delivery Note

(The first transaction links to Invoice; the second transaction links to Purchase Order; the third transaction links to Delivery Note.)

Test your understanding 2

	a) Credit Sale	b) Cash Sale
Net	£3,000	£2,800
VAT	£600	£560
Gross	£3,600	£3,360

Workings:

a) 3,600 ÷ 120 x 100 = 3,000

   3,600 ÷ 120 x 20 = 600

b) 2,800 ÷ 100 x 20 = 560

   2,800 ÷ 100 x 120 = 3,360

Test your understanding 3

Invoice 1 – The cost of the paper towels is £298.88.

Invoice 2 – £250.00 × 20/100 = £50.00. Therefore the VAT would be £50.

Invoice 3 – £480.00/1.2 = £400. £480 - £400 = £80.00. Therefore the VAT would be £80.

 Test your understanding 4

INVOICE

Invoice to:
St Peter's Secondary School
141 St Petersgate
Manchester
M2 6KS

How Two Ltd
1 Baker Street
London
WC1 8QT

Tel: 0207 890 1234
Fax: 0207 890 1235

Deliver to:

As above

Invoice no: 95157
Tax point: 3rd November 17
VAT reg no: 618 2201 63
Delivery note no: 1114
Account no: SPS 1124

Code	Description	Quantity	VAT rate	Unit price	Amount net of VAT
			%	£	£
SMG 121	Samsong HD Monitor	5	20	69.99	349.95
SMG 123	Samsong HD Monitor	12	20	129.99	1,559.88
SMG 124	Samsong HD Monitor	8	20	149.99	1,199.92
					3,109.75
Bulk discount 15%					(466.46)
					2,643.29
VAT					528.65
Total amount payable					3,171.94

Test your understanding 5

Cavalier Beds
3 Brussels Road
County Road
Gloucester
GL6 6TH
Tel: 01456 698271   Fax: 01456 698272

Invoice to:		Invoice no:	67895
		Date:	28/10/X6
KP Furniture Ltd 9 Paris Street COLCHESTER CF25 1XY		VAT reg no:	488 7922 26
		Delivery note no:	6785
		Account no:	KP12

Code		Quantity	VAT rate	Unit price £	Amount excl of VAT £
MAT15K	Deluxe Mattress	5	20%	98.00	490.00

Trade discount 10%	49.00
Subtotal	441.00
VAT	88.20
Total amount payable	529.20

Test your understanding 6

Goods Received Note

Goods Received Note		
GRN number: 124		
Date goods received: 31st October 20X7		
Delivery note number: 2212		
Received From:		
Tablet World		
477 High Street		
Oxford		
OX10 5WD		
Quantity	**Code**	**DESCRIPTION**
15	SSX52	**Samsung SX52 9" Tablet computers**
15	DL656	**Dall MC656 8" Tablet computers**

Received by: *JESSICA HOWARD* ....

Signature: *J. Howard*............ Date: *31st October 2017*..........

 Case study activity 17

	Document
Sent by the customer (How Two Ltd) to state which goods they want to purchase	**A purchase order**
Sent by the supplier to How Two Ltd with the goods when despatched	**A delivery note**
Sent by the supplier to How Two Ltd to inform them of how much the goods cost	**A sales invoice**

Case study activity 18

Delivery Note:

Delivery Note	
To: Redshaw Cables 17 High Street Manchester M1 6RS	**From: How Two Ltd.** 1 Baker Street London WC1 8QT

Delivery Address:
Four Lane Ends
New Mills
SK22 4LG

Delivery note: 1027
Date of issue: 29th October 20X7
Purchase order number: PO1562

Delivery date: 30th October 20X7

Quantity	Code	DESCRIPTION
20	HDMI62	HDMI Cables
5	ESXA14	Epsan SXA projectors

Received by: ....

Signature: .... Date: ....

 Case study activity 19

Date	Customer	Reference	Invoice No	Total £	VAT £	Net £
26 Nov 2017	G Thomas	TH02	5698	300.72	50.12	250.60

 Case study activity 20

This invoice is sent from King and Co who must be the supplier of the goods. Therefore, this is an invoice received by How Two Ltd from a supplier and should be entered into the **purchases day book**.

Checking documentation

Introduction

In the previous chapter we looked at the different types of business documentation used by a bookkeeper and the purposes for each. Here, we will look at the importance of ensuring that these documents are accurate. We will compare documents in the purchasing process to ensure that they are accurate.

We will also look at the different types of errors that could occur and what action should be taken should this happen.

KNOWLEDGE	CONTENTS
Apply business procedures to sales and purchases	1 Business procedures
	2 Checking documents
3.1 Business procedures for sales and procedures	3 Summary and further questions

1 Business procedures

1.1 Case study: an introduction

 Case study

Jessica has been working on processing sales and purchasing documentation for a few days now and feels as though she is really starting to understand the systems and processes around this.

Her manager is now taking her into the next phase of her training which involves her checking different business documents for accuracy. In doing this it is vital that Jessica understands the importance of checking all business documentation before processing it. She also needs to know what to do if she discovers discrepancies or errors.

1.2 The need to follow business procedures

It is essential to follow business procedures when dealing with sales and purchases to ensure that the processes are completed fully and accurately as required by the organisation. Failure to do so could result in deadlines being missed, which ultimately causes issues for the business.

For example, if goods are not checked properly upon receipt this could lead to the company creating a goods received note for incorrect items of stock and they could be charged incorrectly for items that they have never received.

If there are many queries raised in relation to goods received, this could lead to further complications when it comes to the payment run, and could result in the internal deadline being missed. If this was the case, the supplier may not receive their payment on time which could damage the business relationship with the supplier.

It is important to follow the correct procedures for the following reasons:

- It helps to avoid errors – if the process of completing business documents is followed properly, the number of errors made will be minimal. If errors are made in paying suppliers, i.e. the business overpays them or makes duplicate payments to the supplier, this could lead to cash flow problems for the business. As a result, the business may find that they don't have enough money to pay their suppliers and could therefore have to source money from elsewhere (e.g. a loan or overdraft). This is an expensive option for the business and could have a negative effect on the overall profit or loss.

- It helps to avoid missing internal or external deadlines – this is key to the smooth operation of the sales and purchasing departments. If deadlines are missed, a backlog of work will be created. If you get behind with your work, you could rush to try to get back on top of it which creates a risk of errors being made.

- It ensures processes are completed as required by the business – every business has different needs and requirements from business documents. Invoices, credit notes, purchase orders, delivery notes, goods returned notes and goods received notes will look different depending on the company that has created them. The basic information within these documents however, will remain the same.

- It maintains good business relationships with customers and suppliers – if procedures are followed accurately then the number of errors or queries will be minimal, payments will be made on time and therefore business relationships will remain positive. For example, if a supplier is underpaid, this could lead to them refusing to process any further orders of inventory. If this was the case, there could be delays with fulfilling customer orders therefore this would have a negative impact on both the customer and supplier relationship.

1.3 Ensuring procedures are followed correctly

Following procedures correctly is of paramount importance to the smooth operation of an organisation.

The following steps give you an idea of how to ensure that you are performing work-related tasks correctly to prevent wasting time tracing and correcting errors.

- Ensure that business documentation is completed fully and accurately – make sure that all quantities, prices and discounts are cross checked for accuracy and that all item codes, customer or supplier codes and document reference number e.g. PO numbers or delivery note numbers are correct too.

- Complete all documents on time – within the sales and purchasing departments there will be deadlines that need to be met. It is highly likely that someone else within the department is relying on the completion of your work before they can complete theirs. Failure to meet deadlines will cause delays in sales invoices being sent out to the customer and therefore will delay the payment coming in from the customer. It could also create delays in payments to suppliers which could cause issues in terms of receiving stock to fulfil customer orders. This will have a negative effect of business relationships with both customers and suppliers.

- Ensure that the correct authorisation has been obtained – not having the correct authorisation before sending out documents or processing documentation can lead to errors being made within the system. Obtaining authorisation means that your work has been checked and it has been agreed with someone more senior who has the ability to make business decisions. Failure to do so could lead to incorrect information being entered into the accounts.

An overstatement or understatement of figures within the accounting records could lead to incorrect profit or loss figures being recorded. It is imperative that this is accurate for accurate business decisions to be made. For example, if a profit figure is overstated, the director could start thinking about expansion plans for the business. If the business doesn't have the correct resource to be able to put this into place then this could lead the business to fail.

Test your understanding 1

Which ONE of the following is a likely outcome of procedures NOT being followed correctly?

	✓
Deadlines being met	
Greater customer satisfaction	
Increased profits	
Errors when completing documentation and/or payments	

---

2 Checking documents

2.1 Common errors and discrepancies

If there are errors when checking purchasing documentation, it depends on what the error is as to how it should be dealt with.

There are many different errors or discrepancies that may be found when checking documents but the main ones that you will come across on an invoice might include:

- calculation errors
- incorrect VAT calculations

- incorrect type/quantity of goods
- incorrect prices being charged for the goods.

If this is the case then the invoice should be rejected and a dispute raised with the supplier.

Another common example of discrepancies involves the goods themselves. If the goods are damaged or the incorrect goods have been delivered then the buyer will return the goods to the supplier with a goods returned note, requesting a credit note to be issued from the supplier. Upon receipt of the credit note, the buyer would need to check the goods returned note against the credit note to make sure that there are no discrepancies.

The following information should be checked:

- Do the purchase order numbers match?

- Do the details of the goods returned match, including, the quantity, price and description?

- Have the same % of discounts been applied to the credit note?

- Has the VAT been calculated correctly?

If an error or discrepancy is discovered on a credit note or goods returned note, the issue should be raised and the credit note should not be recorded or processed in the accounts.

Test your understanding 2

Which of the following should be checked on documentation relating to sales and purchases to identify potential errors? (Tick ALL correct answers).

	✓
Purchase Order number	
Quantity of goods supplied	
Prices of goods supplied	
VAT calculation on goods supplied	
Registered charity no of supplier	
Company logo of supplier	
Discount given by supplier	

2.2   Case study: an example of checking documents

 Case study

Jessica has been asked to check the following documentation to see whether there are any discrepancies.

PURCHASE ORDER				

How Two Ltd.
1 Baker Street
London
WC1 8QT
Tel: 0207 3972 226

Date: 25th October 20X7
Purchase order no: PO1671

To:
MMC Direct
12 Saunders Street
London, WC4 VCV
Tel: 0207 3972 226

Delivery address
(if different from above)

As above

Product	Ref	Quantity	Price per unit (excl. VAT) £	Total (excl. VAT) £
Koduk SNS200 Printer	SNS200	10	99.99	999.99
Koduk SNS400 Printer	SNS400	15	149.99	2,249.85
Epsan EPS500 Printer	EPS500	20	109.00	2,810.00
Signed:	*A Khan* Purchasing Manager			

Delivery Note:

Delivery Note		
To: How Two Ltd.	**From:** MMC Direct	
1 Baker Street	12 Saunders Street	
London	London	
WC1 8QT	WC4 VCV	

Delivery note: 2331   **Date of issue:** 30th October 20X7
Purchase order number: PO1671

Delivery Address:
12 Saunders Street
London
WC4 VCV

Delivery date: 31st October 20X7

Quantity	Code	DESCRIPTION
15	SNS201	Koduk SNS201 Printer
10	SNS400	Koduk SNS400 Printer
15	EPS500	Epsan EPS500 Printer

Received by: ....

Signature: ....   Date: ....

Goods Received Note:

Good Received Note		
Received From:		
MMC Direct		
12 Saunders Street		
London		
WC4 VCV		

Delivery note number: 2333
Purchase order number: PO1671

Quantity	Code	DESCRIPTION
15	SNS200	Koduk SNS200 Printer
10	SNS400	Koduk SNS400 Printer
15	EPS500	Epsan EPS500 Printer

Received by: *YACOB SOLVEZ*...

Signature: *Y. Solvez*...............   Date: *31st October 2017*..........

When checking the documents for accuracy the following errors have been identified:

- When checking the calculations of prices on the PO the total price for the Epsan EPS500 Printer is incorrect. The order states 20 @ £109.00 which equals £2,180.00. The total price on the order has been entered as £2,810. This has been signed by A Khan (Purchasing Manager) to say that it is correct.

- The incorrect quantities have been delivered.

  The PO states:

  - 10 x Koduk SNS200 Printers
  - 15 x Koduk SNS400 Printers
  - 20 x Epsan EPS500 Printers

  The delivery note states:

  - 15 x Koduk SNS201 Printers
  - 10 x Koduk SNS400 Printers
  - 15 x Epsan EPS500 Printers

- Some incorrect items have also been delivered. How Two Ltd. ordered 10 x Koduk SNS200 Printers but 15 x Koduk SNS201 Printers have been delivered.

- The supplier address has been entered as the delivery address on the delivery note. This should be the address of How Two Ltd.

- Yacob Solvez has completed a GRN even though the items delivered do not match the PO.

- Yacob has entered the delivery note number incorrectly on the GRN which will cause issues when dealing with the queries.

- On the GRN Yacob states that 15 x Koduk SNS200 Printers have been received when in actual fact it was 15 x Koduk SNS201 Printers. This is the wrong item and therefore should not be accepted. If he has signed to say that the correct item has been received this could cause issues when raising a query with the supplier.

As all of the above is incorrect, this should be referred back to the Purchasing Manager to resolve.

3 Summary and further questions

In this chapter we have looked at how invoices should be checked in business. You should now be able to check the relevant purchasing documentation for errors and you should understand why this is important. You should know what to do if you discover any discrepancies within a place of work and how these should be dealt with.

We will return to the How Two Ltd case study to further practice checking documentation.

Case study activity 21

Jessica has been asked to review the following price list and check whether the Purchase Order has been completed correctly.

She has then been asked to check the additional documentation to see whether there are any discrepancies between the PO, delivery note and GRN.

Price List		
Item description	**Item Code**	**Price (excluding VAT)**
HT Notebook	HT477	345.00
Dall Notepad	DL90X	350.00
Tashibo Note Perfect	TNP450	295.00
Micrasaft Touch Pro	MTP225	399.00

PURCHASE ORDER

How Two Ltd.

1 Baker Street

London

WC1 8QT

Tel: 0207 890 1234

Date: 29th October 20X7
Purchase order no: P01682

To: Tech Unlimited 427 Lever Street Manchester, M1 2LF Tel: 0161 484 7711	Delivery address (if different from above) **As above**

Product	Ref	Quantity	Price per unit (excl. VAT) £	Total (excl. VAT) £
HT Notebook	HT477	5	354.00	1,770.00
Micrasaft Touch Pro	MTP225	7	399.00	2,793.00
Dall Notepad	DL90X	8	350.00	2,400.00
Signed:	*A Khan* Purchasing Manager			

Delivery Note:

	Delivery Note	

To: How Two Ltd.
1 Baker Street
London
WC1 8QT

From: Tech Unlimited
427 Lever Street
Manchester
M1 2LF

Delivery note: 2401
Purchase order number: PO1682

Date of issue: 31st Oct 20X7

Delivery Address:
1 Baker Street
London
WC1 8QT

Delivery date: 1st November 20X7

Quantity	Code	DESCRIPTION
5	HT478	HT Notebook
8	MTP225	Micrasaft Touch Pro
7	DL90X	Dall Notepad

Received by: ....

Signature: .... Date: ....

Goods Received Note:

	Good Received Note	

Received From:
MMC Direct
12 Saunders Street
London
WC4 VCV

Delivery note number: 2401
Purchase order number: PO1682

Quantity	Code	DESCRIPTION
5	HT477	HT Notebook
7	MTP225	Micrasaft Touch Pro
8	DL90X	Dall Notepad

Received by: *YACOB SOLVEZ*...

Signature: *Y. Solvez*............... Date: *31st October 2017*..........

Case study activity 22

Jessica has been asked to review the following goods received note and check whether the invoice has been completed correctly.

Good Received Note				
How Two Ltd. 1 Baker Street London WC1 8QT VAT Number: 231 7787 543		**Received From:** **MMC Direct** 12 Saunders Street London WC4 VCV		
Goods received note number: 1023 **Purchase order number:** PO193 Date: 31st October 2017				
Quantity	**Code**	**DESCRIPTION**		**£**
1	HT477	HT Notebook		225.00
2	MTP225	Micrasaft Touch Pro		500.00
1	DL90X	Dall Notepad		200.00
Received by: *YACOB SOLVEZ* .... Signature: *Y. Solvez*................ Date: *31st October 2017*				

Invoice			
To: **How Two Ltd.** 1 Baker Street London WC1 8QT		**From:** MMC Direct 12 Saunders Street London WC4 VCV	
Date: 5th November 2017			
Invoice number: INV440			
Purchase order number: PO182			
Quantity	**Code**	**DESCRIPTION**	**£**
1	HT477	HT Notebook	225.00
1	MTP225	Micrasaft Touch Pro	500.00
1	DL90X	Dall Notepad	200.00
		Net	925.00
		VAT	155.00
		Total	1,080.00

Answers to chapter activities

Test your understanding 1

	✓
Deadlines being met	
Greater customer satisfaction	
Increased profits	
Errors when completing documentation and/or payments	✓

Test your understanding 2

	✓
Purchase Order number	✓
Quantity of goods supplied	✓
Prices of goods supplied	✓
VAT calculation on goods supplied	✓
Registered charity no of supplier	
Company logo of supplier	
Discount given by supplier	✓

Case study activity 21

The following errors and discrepancies can be identified:

- The HT Notebook has been priced at £354 on the purchase order instead of £345.

- The total of the HT Notebooks should be £1,725 if the correct price of £345 had been stated however £1,770 has been entered on the PO.

- The total of the Dall notepads should be £2,800 but £2,400 has been entered on the PO.

- The incorrect product code has been entered on the delivery note for the HT Notebook.

- The incorrect quantities have been entered on the delivery note for the Micrasaft Touch Pro and the Dall Notepad, 7 Micrasaft Touch Pros had been ordered but the delivery note states 8 have been delivered and 8 Dall Notepads had been ordered but the delivery note states that 7 have been delivered.

- The goods received note matches the purchase order but due to the discrepancies on the delivery note this does not match the goods received note.

 Case study activity 22

The following errors and discrepancies can be identified:

- The incorrect purchase order number has been stated on the invoice

- The incorrect product code has been stated on the invoice for the HP Notebook, this should be HT477 not HP477

- The goods received note states that 2 Micrasaft Touch Pros have been received but only one has been invoiced for.

- 2 Micrasaft Touch Pros have been received which in total come to £500. Only 1 has been entered on the invoice but the price still states £500 which if the price for 2.

- The VAT has been calculated incorrectly on the invoice. It should be £185 not £155.

- The total of the invoice is incorrect, this should be £1,110 not £1,080.

Recording receipts and payments

Introduction

So far, we have looked at the process of making sales and purchases in business and the documentation required to do this. Finally we are going to look at the way in which receipts and payments are recorded and the different methods of receiving or paying money.

KNOWLEDGE	CONTENTS
Apply business procedures to sales and purchases 3.1 Business procedures for sales and procedures	1 Receipts and payments 2 Recording income and expenditure 3 Summary and further questions

1 Receipts and payments

1.1 Case study: an introduction

 Case study

Jessica is coming to the end of her training weeks and is really enjoying her role. She is keen to see the whole process through and has asked her manager whether she can have an insight into how the receipts and payments are recorded.

Her manager is really pleased that she is showing initiative and is keen to learn. He is going to take her through the process and then let her have a go herself but has told her not to process anything until it has been checked by him.

1.2 Cash receipts and payments

There are many different ways a business can make and receive payments. A lot of businesses make electronic payments; however, many customers still pay in cash or by writing a cheque. When physical payments are received by an organisation, the monies will need to be paid into the business's bank account.

In a cash sale or purchase, the transaction is much simpler. The customer will probably place an order verbally and payment is always made as soon as the customer receives the goods or services. Payment for cash sales or purchases are usually made by cash, credit or debit card.

The customer will need a copy of the sales receipt in case they need to return them to the supplier.

 Definition

Monies – A term used to describe all types of payments and receipts including cash, cheques and direct bank transfers.

1.3   Paying-in slips

All business organisations are provided with a paying-in book by the bank. Each paying-in book contains paying-in slips. When money is received from customers in cash or by cheque, it is paid into the bank and is accompanied by one of the completed paying-in slips.

If your job is to pay money into the bank, you will need to complete and sign the bank paying-in slip taken from the paying-in book. The paying-in slip is then given to the bank cashier who will check it against the monies being paid in to the bank.

1.4   Example of a paying-in slip

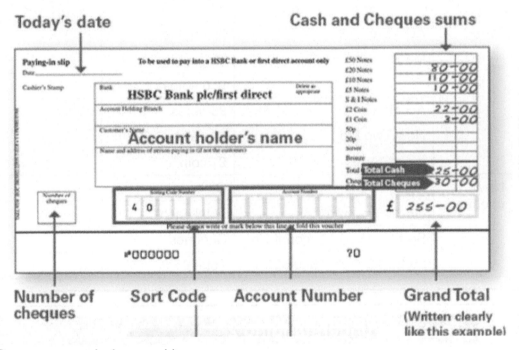

(Source: www.hsbc.co.uk)

1.5   Paying-in requirements and records

You only need to enter the number of cheques being paid in and the total amount on the front of the paying in slip. On the back of the paying in slip you should write a list of the cheques being paid in.

The paying-in stub is the part of the paying-in slip which stays in the paying-in book and is a record for the organisation of the amounts paid into the bank. Sometimes a business may keep a separate list of monies received so that they can cross reference it the bank statement to ensure the correct amount has been paid in, or with the paying in slip should issues arise further on down the line.

Test your understanding 1

Today's date is 19 November 2017.

Jessica has been asked to complete a bank paying-in slip for the money received today, which is as follows:

Notes	Coins	Cheques
3 x £20 notes	25 x £1 coins	Thomas £1,500.00
15 x £10 notes	8 x 50p coins	Friebe £ 750.00
20 x £5 notes	20 x 10p coins	

Complete the paying-in slip below:

Date:	ABC Bank plc Manchester	£50 notes	
		£20 notes	
		£10 notes	
	Account How Two Ltd	£5 notes	
		£2 coin	
		£1 coin	
No of cheques	Paid in by *Jessica Howard*	Other coin	
		Total cash	
	Sort Code Account No	Cheques	
	25-22-78 30087251	Total £	

 Test your understanding 2

Why is it important that the paying-in slip is dated and signed?

1.6 The use of cheques

When a person (or organisation) writes a cheque they are instructing their bank to transfer a specified amount of money from their bank account to the bank account of the recipient of the cheque – the payee.

If the cheque hasn't been completed correctly the bank may return it to the payee. The payee will then have to ask for a replacement cheque from the organisation.

As this causes delays in the payment process, it is important that the cheque is completed correctly in the first place.

1.7 Cheque requirements

For a cheque to be valid it should include:

- **Payee name** The payee is the person or organisation to whom the cheque is written. The payee's name should exactly match the name on their bank account.

- **Date** The date that the cheque is written must include the day, month and the year. A cheque that is more than 6 months old is invalid and the bank will not accept the cheque.

- **Words** The pounds part of the amount being paid must be written in words but the pence part can be written in numbers. If the amount is a whole number of pounds then you should write 'ONLY' after the amount to prevent someone changing the figure.

- **Numbers** The amount being paid should be written in numbers in the box on the right hand side of the cheque. The amount in numbers should exactly match the amount written in words.

- **Signature** The cheque should be signed by an authorised signatory of the organisation.

 Definition

Signatories – a person or persons who are authorised to sign cheques on behalf of an organisation.

Example

ABC Bank PLC	Date: 30th January 20X7
Payee: *Mr John Smith*	
	£350.00
Three hundred and fifty pounds only	MISS ANNE JONES

CHEQUE NO	SORT CODE	ACCOUNT NO
00017	32-32-68	5552222

Test your understanding 3

Today's date is 29th November 2017 and Jessica has been given the following cheques to complete.

Fill in the gaps using the correct numbers, words and/or date.

Cheque A

ABC Bank PLC	Date: 29th November, 2017
Payee: *NB Solutions Ltd*	
Five hundred pounds ONLY	on behalf of How Two Ltd
	J Howard

CHEQUE NO	SORT CODE	ACCOUNT NO
04312	25-22-78	30087251

Cheque B

ABC Bank PLC	Date: 29th November, 2017
Payee: *Armistead & Co*	
	250.50
	on behalf of How Two Ltd
	J Howard

CHEQUE NO	SORT CODE	ACCOUNT NO
04313	25-22-78	30087251

Cheque C

ABC Bank PLC	Date:
Payee: *Mr P Sagan*	
	25.20
Twenty five pounds and 20p only	on behalf of How Two Ltd
	J Howard

CHEQUE NO	SORT CODE	ACCOUNT NO
04314	25-22-78	30087251

Test your understanding 4

Cheques can be signed by anyone in an organisation. True or False?

1.8 Direct debits and standing orders

A **direct debit** is an electronic payment set up by you. You instruct your bank or building society to allow a third party to take money from your bank account at a specified time.

The amounts paid could vary in amount but you will have been informed of how much this will be and when the money will be taken, by the company you are making payment to.

An example of this might be when you are paying your gas or electric bill. The total of the bill will vary from month on month depending on how much gas and electric you use; however, you will have been sent the bill in advance of the money being taken from your bank and this will advise you of the date on which the money will be taken.

A **standing order** is where you set up a regular automated payment to be taken from your bank at a specified time in the month e.g. the 1st of every month. With a standing order, the amounts to be paid are fixed for a certain amount of time. An example of this might be when you are paying your rent. Payments of rent will be the same amount to be paid at the same time each month, in this case, a standing order would be the most suitable method of payment. Standing orders can be amended or cancelled at any time.

Usually, a business will have a direct debit or standing order schedule set up which is basically list of payments that they are expecting to go out of their bank account. This helps them to cross reference payments on their bank statement to ensure the correct ones have been made.

1.9 BACS and faster payments

A **BACS** payment is an automated system that is used to make payment from one bank to another. They are mainly used for direct debits so once you have given permission for an organisation to take payment from your bank account, they will usually do this via the BACS system. A BACS payment takes 3 days to clear in a bank account so if payment was made on Monday, it wouldn't appear in the recipient's bank until Wednesday.

A **faster payment** is an electronic payment that can be made online via internet banking or over the phone. A faster payment is usually made within two hours of making the payment meaning that the money will clear in the recipient's bank account the same day. Both banks have to be part of the faster payments service for this method of payment to be an option however nowadays this is a common service used by businesses to make quick payments to suppliers of goods or services.

Test your understanding 5

Match the definitions with the correct words used in banking

A person who is authorised to sign documents on behalf of an organisation	payee
The person or organisation to whom the cheque is written	stub
A written instruction to transfer a specified sum of money from one bank account to another.	monies
The part of a cheque or paying-in slip kept as a record of the transaction	signatory
The term used to describe different forms of payments and receipts including cash, cheques and direct bank transfers.	cheque

---

2 Recording income and expenditure

2.1 The cash book

 Definition

The Cash Book records receipts and payment made by cash, cheque, credit or debit card, or bank transfer.

One of the most important books used within a business is the cash book. There are various forms of cash book, a 'two column' and a 'three column' cash book.

A two column cash book records details of cash and bank transactions separately as shown here:

CASH BOOK

Date	Details	Bank	Cash	Date	Details	Bank	Cash
		£	£			£	£
		Receipts	.			Payments	

Notes

- The left hand side of the cash book represents the debit side – money received.

- The right hand side of the cash book represents the credit side – money paid out.

- In practice, there is usually a column on both the debit and the credit side for the date.

- The details column describes the transactions – typically the name of the customer and supplier.

- The bank column on the debit side represents money received (by cheque or other bank payment) whereas the bank column on the credit side represents money paid (by cheque or other bank payment).

Some organisations keep separate cash books to record receipts and payments. These are known as the Cash Receipts Book and Cash Payments Book, respectively.

Test your understanding 6

Complete the sentences below using the most appropriate option from the pick list provided.

The _____ is used to record invoices from customers.

The _____ is used to record invoices to suppliers.

The _____ is used to record monies received from customers.

The _____ is used to record monies paid to suppliers.

Pick List

Cash receipts book	Sales day book
Purchases day book	Cash payments book

Test your understanding 7

Alba works in the accounts department at NB Solutions Ltd. She has been asked to complete a two column cash book by recording transactions from today.

For each of the following, indicate whether they should be on the left or right hand side of the Cash Book.

	Left / right
Money received	
Money paid out	
Credit	
Debit	
£220 cash to pay for catering at NB Solutions event	
Bank transfer from a one-off customer for £150	
Cheque from Miss B Craven for £232	
Cheque payable to How Two Ltd for £459	

3 Summary and further questions

In this chapter we have looked at different payment methods and terminology used in sales and purchasing. You should also be able to record the receipts and payments into the cash book appropriately.

We will now return to the How Two Ltd case study to apply this knowledge.

 Case study activity 23

Jessica has been asked to set up the following payments. For each one indicate the best method of payment from the pick list provided.

Payment	Payment method
The telephone bill for calls and line rental for the Manchester office, for which the statement is paid in full on 15th of each month.	
A fixed monthly fee of £3,750, paid on 1st of each month, to Platinum Property Management for rent of the Liverpool offices.	
An urgent payment for £75 to a local contractor who is performing decorating and maintenance work in Reading, but will not work until paid.	
A refund to a small business who placed an order in error and do not have account terms with How Two Ltd. They have written to request the refund.	

Pick list

Cheque

Faster payment bank transfer

Direct debit

Standing order

Case study activity 24

Jessica has received the following three cheques in the week ended 20 November 20X7. Today is 20 November 20X7.

Are the cheques valid? Jessica needs to explain to her manager why easy is either suitable or unsuitable to take to the bank.

Cheque A

ABC Bank PLC	Date: 20th November, 2016

Payee: *How Two Ltd*

	320.00
Three hundred and twenty pounds only	M Salinger
	M Salinger

CHEQUE NO	SORT CODE	ACCOUNT NO
00073	27-60-85	5921434

Cheque B

Plunketts Bank, Wiston	Date: 18th November, 2017

Payee: *How Two Ltd*

	60.99
Sixty pounds & eighty-nine pence only	V Rogers, VCR Ltd
	Vic Rogers

CHEQUE NO	SORT CODE	ACCOUNT NO
02312	56-22-99	7421232

Cheque C

Royston Bank Ltd	Date: 16th November, 2017

Payee: *NB Solutions Ltd*

	406.00
Four hundred and six pounds only	on behalf of N B Solutions Ltd
	O Smart

CHEQUE NO	SORT CODE	ACCOUNT NO
621001	40-08-09	6174931

Case study activity 25

Jessica has been asked to record the following receipts and payments into the cash book:

Receipts:

Cash sale 2nd November £100.

Cash sale 3rd November £80.

Cheque from IT Geeks on the 3rd November £550.

Cheque from NB Solutions on the 4th November £225.

Payments:

Cash purchase on the 2nd November £50.

Cheque paid to MMC Ltd. on the 3rd November £450.

Cheque paid to RBC Plc. On the 4th November £340.

Cash purchase on the 5th November £65.

Cash Book					
Date	**Details**	**Amount**	**Date**	**Details**	**Amount**

Answers to chapter activities

 Test your understanding 1

Date:	ABC Bank plc		£50 notes	
19/11/17	Manchester		£20 notes	60.00
			£10 notes	150.00
	Account		£5 notes	100.00
	How Two Ltd		£2 coin	
			£1 coin	25.00
No of cheques:	Paid in by		Other coin	6.00
	J Howard		Total cash	341.00
2	Sort Code	Account No	Cheques	2250.00
	25-22-78	30087251	Total £	2591.00

 Test your understanding 2

The paying-in slip must be dated and signed so that the bank cashier can contact the person who paid in the money in to the bank, in case there are any queries.

 Test your understanding 3

Cheque A

The amount needs to be included, in numbers – in this case 500.00.

ABC Bank PLC	Date: 29th November, 2017
Payee: *NB Solutions Ltd*	
	500.00
Five hundred pounds ONLY	on behalf of How Two Ltd
	J Howard

CHEQUE NO	SORT CODE	ACCOUNT NO
04312	25-22-78	30087251

Cheque B

The amount needs to be included in written form.

ABC Bank PLC	Date: 29th November, 2017
Payee: *Armistead & Co*	
	250.50
Two hundred and fifty pounds and 50p	on behalf of How Two Ltd
	J Howard

CHEQUE NO	SORT CODE	ACCOUNT NO
04313	25-22-78	30087251

Cheque C

The date needs to be included, to state the day, month and year.

ABC Bank PLC	Date: **29th November, 2017**
Payee: *Mr P Sagan*	
	25.20
Twenty five pounds and 20p only	on behalf of How Two Ltd
	J Howard

CHEQUE NO	SORT CODE	ACCOUNT NO
04314	25-22-78	30087251

Test your understanding 4

The statement is false.

Cheques can only be signed by authorised signatories.

Test your understanding 5

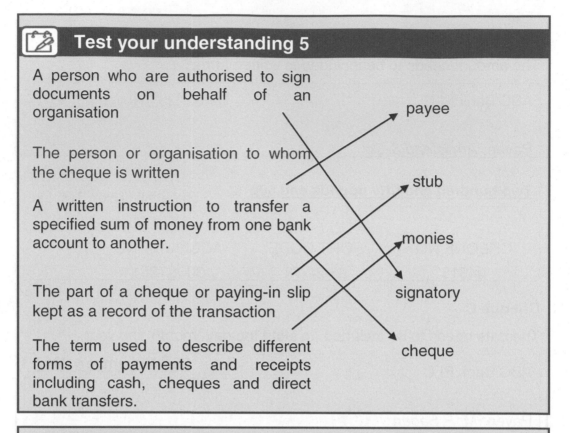

A person who are authorised to sign documents on behalf of an organisation

The person or organisation to whom the cheque is written

A written instruction to transfer a specified sum of money from one bank account to another.

The part of a cheque or paying-in slip kept as a record of the transaction

The term used to describe different forms of payments and receipts including cash, cheques and direct bank transfers.

payee

stub

monies

signatory

cheque

Test your understanding 6

The **Sales day book** is used to record invoices from customers.

The **Purchases day book** is used to record invoices to suppliers.

The **Cash receipts book** is used to record monies received from customers.

The **Cash payments book** is used to record monies paid to suppliers.

Test your understanding 7

	Left / right
Money received	Left
Money paid out	Right
Credit	Right
Debit	Left
£220 cash to pay for catering at NB Solutions event	Right
Bank transfer from a one-off customer for £150	Left
Cheque from Miss B Craven for £232	Left
Cheque payable to How Two Ltd for £459	Right

Case study activity 23

Payment	Payment method
The telephone bill for calls and line rental for the Manchester office, for which the statement is paid in full on 15th of each month.	**Direct debit**
A fixed monthly fee of £3,750, paid on 1st of each month, to Platinum Property Management for rent of the Liverpool offices.	**Standing order**
An urgent payment for £75 to a local contractor who is performing decorating and maintenance work in Reading, but will not work until paid.	**Faster payment bank transfer**
A refund to a small business who placed an order in error and do not have account terms with How Two Ltd. They have written to request the refund.	**Cheque**

 Case study activity 24

Cheque A – the date is incorrect (2016 not 2017), making the cheque invalid

Cheque B – the written value is £60.89 whereas the numerical value of the cheque is £60.99 – these amounts do not match so the cheque is invalid

Cheque C – the cheque is actually made payable to the payer (NB Solutions) rather than the payee. Therefore as the payee is not How Two Ltd, the cheque is not valid.

 Case study activity 25

Cash Book					
Date	**Details**	**Amount**	**Date**	**Details**	**Amount**
2/11	Cash sale	100	2/11	Cash purchase	50
3/11	Cash sale	80	3/11	MMC Ltd.	450
3/11	IT Geeks	550	4/11	RBC Plc.	340
4/11	NB Solutions	225	5/11	Cash purchase	65

Mock Assessment 1 – Access Award in Business Skills

Introduction

The following is a Mock Assessment to be attempted in exam conditions.

You should attempt and aim to complete EVERY task.

Read every task carefully to make sure you understand what is required.

Where the date is relevant, it is given in the task.

Both minus signs and brackets can be used to indicate negative numbers UNLESS task instructions say otherwise.

You must use a full stop to indicate a decimal point.

The assessment includes ten tasks.

Time allowed: 90 minutes

1 Mock Assessment Questions

Task 1 (6 marks)

There are different types of organisation.

a) Complete the following sentence by selecting the most appropriate option from the list of items below each sentence.

An animal welfare organisation is a _____ organisation.

Pick list

- private sector
- public sector
- charitable

b) Show whether this statement is true or false.

Statement	True	False
The primary aim of an organisation in the private sector is to make a profit.		
The public sector is funded by private individuals or organisations		

It is important to understand the role of the accounting department within an organisation.

c) Show whether the following statements are true or false.

Statement	True	False
Information provided by the accounting department is used by external customers only.		
An example of an internal customer of the accounting department is a close friend of one of the managers of the organisation.		
The Human Resources department are responsible for dealing with employee relations and personnel and their payroll.		

Task 2 (3 marks)

At the end of every year your organisation calculates the profit or loss for the year.

a)   Complete the sentence below by selecting the most appropriate option from the following list:

- equals

- is more than

- is less than

When income _____ expenditure this results in a loss.

Last year your organisation recorded income and expenditure as shown in the table below:

Income and expenditure	£
Sales	192,000
Cost of sales	115,200
Premises expenses	25,920
Heat and light	23,040
Administration and wages	15,808

b)   Use the income and expenditure figures to calculate the profit or loss and state whether this is a profit or loss:

Profit/Loss   £ [   ]

Profit/Loss   [   ]

Task 3 (6 marks)

It is important to understand the terminology used when buying and selling goods for cash and on credit.

a) Insert an item from the following pick list into the right hand column of the table below to identify the term described. You will not need to use all of the items.

Description	Term described
A person or organisation who is owed money by the company for purchases made.	
A transaction to sell goods when the payment is made one month later.	

Pick list

A cash sale   A cash purchase   A credit sale

A credit purchase   A debtor/receivable   A creditor/payable

Your organisation purchased 12 packs of printer cartridges at £28.65 per box from MG Stationers.

b) What is the total cost of the printer paper?

Answer: £ [   ]

MG Stationers have asked for immediate payment.

c) Is the purchase of the printer paper a cash transaction or a credit transaction?

Tick the correct answer below.

Type of transaction	✓
Cash transaction	
Credit transaction	

d)   From the picklist below, enter the correct payment term next to the most appropriate statement.

Statement	Payment term
To help the supplier with out of pocket expenses for large orders is a………..	
When a customer pays upon receipt of the goods or services is a…………………	

Picklist

- Payment after invoice date

- Payment at the end of the month of invoice

- Payment in advance

- Payment on delivery

Task 4 (9 marks)

ABC Ltd. wish to purchase 10 x Product S123 and 15 x Product RC557.

The list price of product S123 is £10.99 and the list price for product RC557 is £12.50.

The last purchase order number used was PO12456. ABC Ltd. have agreed 30 day payment terms with XYZ Ltd. VAT is charged at the standard rate of 20% and today's date is 27th November 20X7.

a)   Complete the following purchase order with the following information:

- Customer name

- Supplier name

- PO number

- Product pricing

- Net

- VAT

- Total

Purchase Order

123 High Street

Manchester

M23 1RD

VAT Reg No. 441 3898 00

Telephone Number: 0161 838 9921

To:

Sunnyside

Beach Business Park

LN1 5NQ

Date: 27/11/2017

P.O. Number:

Quantity	Description	Unit Price	Price
10	Product S123	10.99	
15	Product RC557	12.50	
		Net	
		VAT	
		Total	

Payment terms agreed: 30 days

b) Upon receipt of the goods, ABC Ltd. check the details of the purchase order against which of the following documents?

Document Type	✓
Purchase invoice	
Sales invoice	
Delivery note	
Goods received note	

Task 5 (3 marks)

Your organisation keeps detailed records of expenses.

Motor fuel expenses for each of four delivery vehicles are shown in the table below.

a)   Complete the table to show the motor fuel expense for Vehicle 1.

Delivery vehicles	Motor fuel expense £
Vehicle 1	
Vehicle 2	241.12
Vehicle 3	221.90
Vehicle 4	259.58
Total	**974.20**

b)   Calculate the average motor fuel expense per vehicle.

Answer: £ [   ]

Expenses relating to items of stationery are shown in the table below.

c)   Complete the table to show the total stationery expense.

Items	Expense £
Ink cartridges	125.00
Printer paper	119.50
Envelopes	76.80
Pens	53.70
Total	

Task 6 (6 marks)

Your organisation records of sales by store.

Monday's sales for each region are shown in the table below.

a) Complete the table to show the total sales for all stores for Monday.

Region	Sales (£)
Store A	1510.02
Store B	1445.65
Store C	1330.14
Store D	1552.75
Total	

b) Which store made the highest amount of sales?

c) Which store made the lowest amount of sales?

d) What is the range of sales made?

Wages for each of the stores for Monday are shown in the table below.

Region	Wages (£)
Store A	116.77
Store B	119.68
Store C	
Store D	124.22
Total	**467.08**

e) Complete the table to show Monday's wages for Store C

f) Which of the following is the ratio of the total wages to wages for Store A?

Ratio	✔
2:1	
3:1	
4:1	

Task 7 (9 marks)

You have been asked to calculate the annual bonuses for three of the sales staff.

a) Using the information in the table below, calculate the bonuses for employees B, C and D.

Employee	Annual Salary	Bonus calculated as a % of salary	Bonus Payment	Total Pay for the year
A	£25,000	5%	£1,250	£26,250
B	£19,500	10%		
C	£28,000	7.5%		
D	£22,500	5%		

Employee B has performed really well in her role this year and as a result, her manager has awarded her with a pay increase equivalent to 1/5 of her current salary.

b) How much will Employee B receive in respect of her pay increase?

c) What will Employee B's total salary be for next year before any bonus calculations?

d) Based on her new wage, how much should Employee B expect to be paid per month before any tax or national insurance deductions?

Task 8 (6 marks)

a) Identify the most appropriate software to use in each of the situations below.

Situation	Type of software to use			
	Presentation ✓	Word processing ✓	Email ✓	Spreadsheet ✓
Listing the mileage of the sales staff paid at 45p per mile				
Communicating training on the new system to your team				
Communicating a request to take some annual leave				
Communicating with a customer to chase an outstanding debt				

It is important to observe confidentiality.

b) Show whether the following statement is true or false.

Statement	True	False
Information about staff wages should not be held on the computer because it is confidential information.		

c) Complete the following sentence by selecting the most appropriate option from the pick list below.

The addresses of all staff should be accessible to _____.

Pick list

all staff

accounts department staff only

authorised staff only

Task 9 (6 marks)

You have seen a job advertised with an online recruitment agency and feel that you have the correct skills and qualities to be able to apply.

a)   How would you do this?

	✔
Call the company who are recruiting and ask if you can apply directly instead of going through the recruitment agency.	
Complete the online application form and send it off along with your CV.	
Ask your friend to telephone them on your behalf because they sound more intelligent than you.	
Ask your mum to write them a letter with a copy of your CV because she can verify your qualification history.	

b)   You are creating your CV for the first time, which FOUR of the following pieces of information should you include?

	✔
Date of birth	
Hobbies	
Relevant interests and experience	
Employment history	
Marital status	
Current contact details	
How many pets you have	
Qualifications	

It is 10pm and you have just completed your CV and the online application form.

c)   What should you do now?

	✓
Proof read the application form only	
Submit them both straightaway	
Check both documents thoroughly before submitting them	
Save them and send them first thing in the morning as you will probably get a quick response that way	

Task 10 (6 marks)

You have been given the following details of amounts owed to credit suppliers.

Supplier	Payment to be received by supplier	Invoices to be paid	
		Invoice Amount	Invoice date
ABC Ltd.	14 days from invoice date	£145.61	28/09/X7
DEF Ltd.	At the end of the month of invoice date	£454.62	28/09/X7
		£381.79	29/09/X7
KLM Ltd.	30 days after the invoice date	£679.83	2/10/X7
		£654.55	2/10/X7

Complete the table below by inserting the total amount to be paid to each supplier and the by which the supplier should receive their payment.

Supplier	Amount to be paid (£)	Date supplier should receive payment
ABC Ltd.		
DEF Ltd.		
KLM Ltd.		

Mock Assessment 2 – Access Award in Business Skills

Introduction

The following is a Mock Assessment to be attempted in exam conditions.

You should attempt and aim to complete EVERY task.

Read every task carefully to make sure you understand what is required.

Where the date is relevant, it is given in the task.

Both minus signs and brackets can be used to indicate negative numbers UNLESS task instructions say otherwise.

You must use a full stop to indicate a decimal point.

The assessment includes ten tasks.

Time allowed: 90 minutes

1 Mock Assessment Questions

Task 1 (6 marks)

There are different types of organisation.

a) Place a tick in the appropriate column below to show whether each of the organisations listed are in the public sector, private sector, charitable sector, service sector or manufacturing sector.

Organisation	Public Sector	Private Sector	Charitable Sector	Service Sector	Manufact-uring Sector
A retail supermarket					
The local library					
An organisation generating income to support its purpose					
An organisation that makes products to sell					

It is important to understand the role of the accounting department within an organisation.

b) Show whether the following statements are true or false.

Statement	True	False
Information provided by the accounting department is of no interest to anybody else in the organisation		
Customers of the accounting department can be from inside or outside the organisation.		

Task 2 (3 marks)

At the end of every year your organisation calculates the profit or loss for the year.

a) Complete the sentence below by selecting the most appropriate option from the following list:

- equals
- is more than
- is less than

When expenditure _____ income this results in a loss.

Last year your organisation recorded income and expenditure as shown in the table below:

Income and expenditure	£
Sales	163,200
Cost of sales	119,760
Premises expenses	22,032
Heat and light	19,584
Administration and wages	13,437

b) Use the income and expenditure figures to calculate whether you have made a profit or loss and state whether this is a profit or loss:

Profit/Loss £

Profit/Loss

Task 3 (6 marks)

a) Insert an item from the following list into the right hand column of the table below to identify the term described. You will not need to use all of the items.

Description	Term described
A customer who owes an organisation money	
A transaction when an organisation buys goods or services and pays its supplier immediately	
A transaction to purchase goods when payment is made a month later.	
An organisation that is owed money for goods or services supplied.	

Pick list

A cash sale   A cash purchase   A credit sale

A credit purchase   A receivable/ debtor   A payable/ creditor

b) Match each of the following situations to the correct payment term:

A customer places an order and pays for the goods upon receipt of them.	Payment at the end of the month of invoice
A customer purchases some goods and is invoiced on the 10th January. They pay for them on the 31st January.	Payment in advance
A customer purchases some goods and is invoiced on the 17th January. They pay for them on the 31st January.	Payment 14 days after invoice
A customer places a large order and pays for some of it upfront.	Payment on delivery

Task 4 (9 marks)

Sunnyside Ltd. wish to purchase 12 x Hanging Baskets and 18 x Ceramic Plant Pots from Happydays PLC.

The list price of the Hanging Baskets is £17.99 and the list price of the Ceramic Plant Pots is £15.50. The last purchase order number used was PO1090.

Sunnyside Ltd. have agreed 10 day payment terms with Happydays PLC. VAT is charged at the standard rate of 20% and today's date is 28th November 20X7.

a) Complete the following purchase order with the following information:

*   Customer name

*   Supplier name

*   PO number

*   Product pricing

*   Net

*   VAT

*   Total

Purchase Order

476 Laneside Road

Oxford

OX10 5WD

VAT Reg No. 397 8682 00

Telephone Number: 01346 572354

To:

Date: 28/11/2017

P.O. Number:

Wayside Business Park

Taunton

TN5 6NQ

Quantity	Description	Unit Price	Price
12	Hanging Baskets	17.99	
15	Ceramic Plant Pots	15.50	
		Net	
		VAT	
		Total	

Payment terms agreed: 14 days

b) Sunnyside receive an invoice in respect of these goods, which three documents should it be checked against to ensure that there are no errors before the invoice can be processed?

Document Type	✓
Remittance Advice	
Sales invoice	
Delivery note	
Goods received note	
Customer order	
Purchase order	

Task 5 (3 marks)

You work in the accounts team of a retail business with a number of branches in different areas of the UK. You have been asked to produce some calculations in relation to the number of customers that have visited the stores over the last 4 weeks.

You have been given the following information:

Number of customers that have visited each store					
Manchester	London	Liverpool	Newcastle	Edinburgh	Cardiff
825	1,458	984	675	1,020	1,374

a) Arrange the numbers shown above in descending order.

b) Calculate the range for the number of customers visiting the stores.

c) What is the average number of customers visiting the stores during this period?

Task 6 (6 marks)

An organisation is reviewing the selling price of some of its products.

The current selling price of product number AB3 is £89.00. This is to be increased by 8%.

a) Calculate the increase in selling price for product number AB3

Answer: £ [   ]

The current selling price of product number BA8 is £146.00. This is to be increased by 3/8 (three eighths).

b) Calculate the increase in selling price for product number 74

Answer: £ [   ]

Your organisation keeps detailed records of expenses incurred by each vehicle used by the sales team.

c) Complete the table to show the expenses for vehicle registration no R6 HMW

Vehicle Registrations	Expenses (£)
MJ53 FXJ	986.00
BD51 SMT	1,054.90
R6 HMW	
PK63 GNT	3,944.00
Total	**7,062.90**

d) Which of the following is the ratio of the expenses for vehicle registration PK63 GNT to the expenses for vehicle registration MJ53 FXJ? Tick the correct answer.

Ratio	✓
2:1	
3:1	
4:1	

e) If your manager requests expense reports every three months, how often are they required?

Frequency	✓
Daily	
Quarterly	
Monthly	
Annually	

A company has made £1,710,486 in Sales Revenue over the last year.

f) Write this figure in words.

Answer:

Task 7 (9 marks)

You have been asked to calculate the annual bonuses for three of the sales staff.

a) Using the information in the table below, calculate the bonuses for employees B, C and D.

Employee	Annual Salary	Bonus calculated as a % of salary	Bonus Payment	Total Pay for the year
A	£15,000	4%	£1,250	£26,250
B	£12,500	8%		
C	£19,000	10%		
D	£21,500	15%		

Employee B has performed really well in her role this year and as a result, her manager has awarded her with a pay increase equivalent to 1/5 of her current salary.

b) How much will Employee B receive in respect of her pay increase?

c) What will Employee B's total salary be for next year before any bonus calculations?

d) Based on her new wage, how much should Employee B expect to be paid per month before any tax or national insurance deductions?

Task 8 (6 marks)

You work for Markham Products and have been asked to send an email to Martin Dale, your manager, to confirm that you have arranged refreshments for a director's board meeting on 8 August.   You should point out that the refreshments will be served at 10.30am.

Using the items at the bottom of the page, compose an appropriate e-mail in the template below. You will not need to use all of the items.

From: AATstudent@markhamproducts.com	
To:	
Subject:	

I've ordered refreshements	Board meeting: Refreshments	Please accept this email as confirmation that refreshments for the board meeting on 8 August will be served at 10.30am. .	
AAT student	Attendance	The refreshments will be at the meeting on 10 August and will be served at 8.30am.	
Cheers	Hey M	Kind regards,	Hello Martin
mdale@markhamproducts.com		janettebones@kazeekrafts.com	

You have been asked to send a list of tomorrow's deliveries to the warehouse manager. This is a very urgent task as the warehouse manager needs to allocate the deliveries before the end of today.

b)   Select the most appropriate form of communication to accompany the list of deliveries

Option	✔
Letter	
Memo	
email	

It is important to observe confidentiality.

c)   Show whether the following statements are true or false.

Statement	True	False
If a manager asks to see confidential information, you should let them see it		

d)   Complete the following sentence by selecting the most appropriate option from the pick list below.

Confidential information should be _____ if you have to leave your desk.

Pick list

- kept in a locked drawer

- hidden under the computer keyboard

- given to a colleague for safekeeping

Task 9 (6 marks)

Jonathan is looking for a new job.

a)   Jonathan has found a job he wishes to apply for. The following personal qualities have been listed as desirable for the role: flexibility, courtesy and using initiative. He considers his recent experience and finds an example of each. Match the statement with the correct personal skill from the pick list provided.

In Jonathan's previous role as a customer service liaison in the local hotel, he often made himself available at short notice to cover for other staff when they were off sick or wished to take annual leave.	
In Jonathan's previous role, he was responsible for processing the Sales invoices. Before any Sales invoices were allowed to be sent out to the customer, he needed to have them authorised by his manager, Anna. Anna was off sick for the whole week. Nobody told Jonathan who else could authorise them. Jonathan took them to the Sales Director and explained the situation to obtain authorisation from someone else.	
In the customer service role, Jonathan had an elderly couple who checked in one day. They had been allocated a room on the top floor of the hotel and there was no lift. Jonathan change their room to one on the ground floor.	

Pick list

Flexibility   Courtesy   Using initiative

b)   You have seen a job that you want to apply for, which TWO of the following are the best ways to apply?

Actions	✓
Send them a letter	
Send them an email	
Complete an online application and attach your CV	
Send a letter of application along with your CV	
Apply by telephone	

c) State whether the following is true or false.

Your date of birth and marital status should be included on a CV?

	✓
True	
False	

Task 10 (6 marks)

You have been given the following details of amounts owed to credit suppliers.

Supplier	Payment to be received by supplier	Invoices to be paid	
		Invoice Amount	Invoice date
ABC Ltd.	10 days from invoice date	£1,245.75	30/09/X7
DEF Ltd.	At the end of the month of invoice date	£543.82	17/09/X7
		£746.69	28/09/X7
KLM Ltd.	30 days after the invoice date	£986.41	26/09/X7
		£742.53	26/09/X7

Complete the table below by inserting the total amount to be paid to each supplier and the by which the supplier should receive their payment.

Supplier	Amount to be paid (£)	Date supplier should receive payment
ABC Ltd.		
DEF Ltd.		
KLM Ltd.		

Mock Assessment Answers

1 Mock Assessment 1 Answers

Task 1 (6 marks)

There are different types of organisation.

a) An animal welfare organisation is a **charitable** organisation.

b) Show whether this statement is true or false.

Statement	True	False
The primary aim of an organisation in the private sector is to make a profit.	✓	
The public sector is funded by private individuals or organisations		✓

c) Show whether the following statements are true or false.

Statement	True	False
Information provided by the accounting department is used by external customers only.		✓
An example of an internal customer of the accounting department is a close friend of one of the managers of the organisation.		✓
The Human Resources department are responsible for dealing with employee relations and personnel and their payroll.	✓	

Task 2 (3 marks)

a) When income **is less than** expenditure this results in a loss.

b) Use the income and expenditure figures to calculate the profit or loss and state whether this is a profit or loss:

Profit/Loss   £ | 12,032 |

Profit/Loss | **Profit** |

Task 3 (6 marks)

a)

Description	Term described
A person or organisation who is owed money by the company for purchases made.	**A creditor/ payable**
A transaction to sell goods when the payment is made one month later.	**A credit sale**

b) What is the total cost of the printer paper?

Answer: £ 343.80

c)

Type of transaction	✓
Cash transaction	✓
Credit transaction	

d)

Statement	Payment term
To help the supplier with out of pocket expenses for large orders is a………..	**Payment in advance**
When a customer pays upon receipt of the goods or services is a…………………	**Payment on delivery**

Task 4 (9 marks)

a)

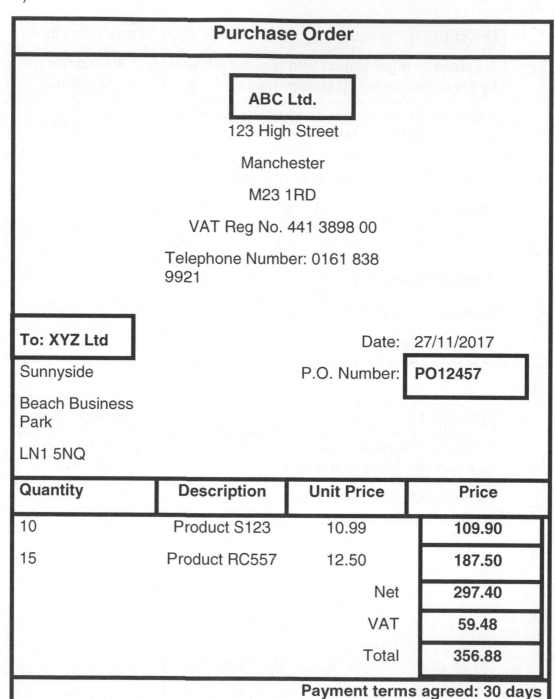

Purchase Order			
	ABC Ltd.		
	123 High Street		
	Manchester		
	M23 1RD		
	VAT Reg No. 441 3898 00		
	Telephone Number: 0161 838 9921		
To: XYZ Ltd		Date: 27/11/2017	
Sunnyside		P.O. Number: **PO12457**	
Beach Business Park			
LN1 5NQ			
Quantity	**Description**	**Unit Price**	**Price**
10	Product S123	10.99	**109.90**
15	Product RC557	12.50	**187.50**
		Net	**297.40**
		VAT	**59.48**
		Total	**356.88**
Payment terms agreed: 30 days			

b)

Document Type	✓
Purchase invoice	
Sales invoice	
Delivery note	✓
Goods received note	

Task 5 (3 marks)

a)

Delivery vehicles	Motor fuel expense
Vehicle 1	251.60

b)   Calculate the average motor fuel expense per vehicle.

Answer: £   243.55

c)

Items	Expense
Ink cartridges	125.00
Printer paper	119.50
Envelopes	76.80
Pens	53.70
Total	375.00

Task 6 (6 marks)

a)

Region	Sales (£)
Store A	1510.02
Store B	1445.65
Store C	1330.14
Store D	1552.75
Total	**5838.56**

b) Which store made the highest amount of sales?

Store D

c) Which store made the lowest amount of sales?

Store C

d) What is the range of sales made?

£222.61

e)

Region	Wages (£)
Store A	116.77
Store B	119.68
Store C	**106.41**
Store D	124.22
Total	**467.08**

f) Which of the following is the ratio of the total wages to wages for Store A?

Ratio	✔
2:1	
3:1	
4:1	✔

Task 7 (9 marks)

a)

Employee	Annual Salary	Bonus calculated as a % of salary	Bonus Payment	Total Pay for the year
A	£25,000	5%	£1,250	£26,250
B	£19,500	10%	£1,950	£21,450
C	£28,000	7.5%	£2,100	£30,100
D	£22,500	5%	£1,125	£23,625

b)   How much will Employee B receive in respect of her pay increase?

£3,900

c)   What will Employee B's total salary be for next year before any bonus calculations?

£23,400

d)   Based on her new wage, how much should Employee B expect to be paid per month before any tax or national insurance deductions?

£1,950

Task 8 (6 marks)

a)

Situation	Type of software to use			
	Presentation ✔	Word processing ✔	Email ✔	Spreadsheet ✔
Listing the mileage of the sales staff paid at 45p per mile				✔
Communicating training on the new system to your team	✔			
Communicating a request to take some annual leave			✔	
Communicating with a customer to chase an outstanding debt		✔		

b) Show whether the following statement is true or false.

Statement	True	False
Information about staff wages should not be held on the computer because it is confidential information.		✔

c) The addresses of all staff should be accessible to **authorised staff only.**

Task 9 (6 marks)

a)

	✓
Call the company who are recruiting and ask if you can apply directly instead of going through the recruitment agency.	
Complete the online application form and send it off along with your CV.	✓
Ask your friend to telephone them on your behalf because they sound more intelligent than you.	
Ask your mum to write them a letter with a copy of your CV because she can verify your qualification history.	

b)

	✓
Date of birth	
Hobbies	
Relevant interests and experience	✓
Employment history	✓
Marital status	
Current contact details	✓
How many pets you have	
Qualifications	✓

c)

	✓
Proof read the application form only	
Submit them both straightaway	
Check both documents thoroughly before submitting them	✓
Save them and send them first thing in the morning as you will probably get a quick response that way	

Task 10 (6 marks)

Supplier	Amount to be paid (£)	Date supplier should receive payment
ABC Ltd.	£145.61	12/10/X7
DEF Ltd.	£836.41	30/09/X7
KLM Ltd.	£1,334.38	1/11/X7

2 Mock Assessment 2 Answers

Task 1 (6 marks)

a)

Organisation	Public Sector	Private Sector	Charitable Sector	Service Sector	Manufact-uring Sector
A retail supermarket		✔			
The local library	✔				
An organisation generating income to support its purpose			✔		
An organisation that makes products to sell					✔

b)

Statement	True	False
Information provided by the accounting department is of no interest to anybody else in the organisation		✔
Customers of the accounting department can be from inside or outside the organisation.	✔	

Task 2 (3 marks)

a) When expenditure **is more than** income this results in a loss.

b)

Profit/Loss   £ | -11,613 |

Profit/Loss | **Loss** |

Task 3 (6 marks)

a)

Description	Term described
A customer who owes an organisation money	**A receivable/ debtor**
A transaction when an organisation buys goods or services and pays its supplier immediately	**A cash sale**
A transaction to purchase goods when payment is made a month later.	**A credit purchase**
An organisation that is owed money for goods or services supplied.	**A payable/ creditor**

b)

A customer places an order and pays for the goods upon receipt of them.	Payment at the end of the month of invoice
A customer purchases some goods and is invoiced on the 10th January. They pay for them on the 31st January.	Payment in advance
A customer purchases some goods and is invoiced on the 17th January. They pay for them on the 31st January.	Payment 14 days after invoice
A customer places a large order and pays for some of it upfront.	Payment on delivery

Task 4 (9 marks)

a)

	Purchase Order		

Sunnyside Ltd

476 Laneside Road

Oxford

OX10 5WD

VAT Reg No. 397 8682 00

Telephone Number: 01346 572354

To: Happydays PLC.

Wayside Business Park

Taunton

TN5 6NQ

Date: 28/11/2017

P.O. Number: **PO1091**

Quantity	Description	Unit Price	Price
12	Hanging Baskets	17.99	**215.88**
15	Ceramic Plant Pots	15.50	**232.50**
		Net	448.38
		VAT	89.67
		Total	538.05

Payment terms agreed: 14 days

b)

Document Type	✓
Remittance Advice	
Sales invoice	
Delivery note	✓
Goods received note	✓
Customer order	
Purchase order	✓

Task 5 (3 marks)

a) Arrange the numbers shown above in descending order.

1,458	1,374	1,020	984	825	675

b) Calculate the range for the number of customers visiting the stores.

783

c) What is the average number of customers visiting the stores during this period?

1,056

Task 6 (6 marks)

a) Calculate the increase in selling price for product number AB3

Answer: £ 7.12

b) Calculate the increase in selling price for product number 74

Answer: £ 54.75

c)

Vehicle Registrations	Expenses (£)
MJ53 FXJ	986.00
BD51 SMT	1,054.90
R6 HMW	**1,078.00**
PK63 GNT	3,944.00
Total	**7,062.90**

d)

Ratio	✓
2:1	
3:1	
4:1	✓

e)

Frequency	✓
Daily	
Quarterly	✓
Monthly	
Annually	

f)

Answer: | **One million seven hundred and ten thousand four hundred and eighty six pounds**

Task 7 (9 marks)

a)

Employee	Annual Salary	Bonus calculated as a % of salary	Bonus Payment	Total Pay for the year
A	£15,000	4%	£1,250	£26,250
B	£12,500	8%	**£1,000**	**£13,500**
C	£19,000	10%	**£1,900**	**£20,900**
D	£21,500	15%	**£3,225**	**£24,725**

b) How much will Employee B receive in respect of her pay increase?

£3,125

c) What will Employee B's total salary be for next year before any bonus calculations?

£15,625

d) Based on her new wage, how much should Employee B expect to be paid per month before any tax or national insurance deductions?

£1,302.08

Task 8 (6 marks)

a)

From: AATstudent@markhamproducts.com
To: mdale@markhamproducts.com
Subject: Board meeting: Refreshments

Hello Martin

Please accept this email as confirmation that refreshments for the board meeting on 8 August will be served at 10.30am.

Kind regards,

AAT student

b)

Option	✓
Letter	
Memo	
email	✓

c)

Statement	True	False
If a manager asks to see confidential information, you should let them see it		✓

d) Confidential information should be **kept in a locked drawer** if you have to leave your desk.

Task 9 (6 marks)

a)

In Jonathan's previous role as a customer service liaison in the local hotel, he often made himself available at short notice to cover for other staff when they were off sick or wished to take annual leave.	**Flexibility**
In Jonathan's previous role, he was responsible for processing the Sales invoices. Before any Sales invoices were allowed to be sent out to the customer, he needed to have them authorised by his manager, Anna. Anna was off sick for the whole week. Nobody told Jonathan who else could authorise them. Jonathan took them to the Sales Director and explained the situation to obtain authorisation from someone else.	**Using initiative**
In the customer service role, Jonathan had an elderly couple who checked in one day. They had been allocated a room on the top floor of the hotel and there was no lift. Jonathan change their room to one on the ground floor.	**Courtesy**

b)

Actions	✓
Send them a letter	
Send them an email	
Complete an online application and attach your CV	✓
Send a letter of application along with your CV	✓
Apply by telephone	

c) Your date of birth and marital status should be included on a CV?

	✓
True	
False	✓

Task 10 (6 marks)

Supplier	Amount to be paid (£)	Date supplier should receive payment
ABC Ltd.	£1,245.75	10th October 20X7
DEF Ltd.	£1,290.51	30th September 20X7
KLM Ltd.	£1,728.94	26th October 20X7

INDEX

V

W

KAPLAN PUBLISHING